The Big Bang – And Jesus Christ Birthed The Universe!

(In The Big Bang: The Sun, the Stars, the Quasi and the Moons Were All Birthed To Reflect the True Light --- Jesus Christ)

Ifeanyi Chukwujama

For more information, go to our websites

www.JesusOn.co

Or

www.ChristianityIsLife.com

Or write to Ifeanyi Chukwujama, 394-396 Warren Street, Boston, Massachusetts 02119.

EDITED BY: Ifeanyi k. Chukwujama

ISBN: 10: 0692206833
ISBN-13: 978-0692206836

DEDICATION

This book is dedicated to God for bringing me to the
light; and for opening me up to this great and wonderful
experience and filling my heart with His knowledge and
His understanding; and for showing me things I never
knew and making me understand them.
And also to the memory of my father Enoch for teaching
me that humility is the best human virtue; and my
mother, Victoria for her love, tireless care and industry.
And also to my wife, Ukamaka, for her special love and
support; and for making life's journey with me through
thick and thin, and emerging with me at the other end
of the tunnel.
And also to my children Ifeanyi Jr., Chiamaka, Ifenna
and Chukwunonso for their love, inspiration and
insights. They have all been a very important part of my
life's journey, and together with my wife, played vital
roles in helping me shape my thoughts and find
meaning for a great majority of the things revealed to
me by God as I wrote this book.
And also to my extended family who loved and
supported me and helped bolster my sense of worth
when I had nothing; and to a countless others, who
made contributions to my life, big or small. Everything is
important, because together they determine our
directions in life and who we ultimately become.
And also to you, the reader, because you are important
to our Lord Jesus Christ. Experience Him and live!
Glory be to God.

Ifeanyi Chukwujama

CONTENTS

ACKNOWLEDGMENTS

Our God is great. And our Lord Jesus Christ is great, because He is one with the Father. He is faithful in all He has promised. I am a living example of His unfading love, His great mercy, His abundant grace, and His unlimited providence. The Bible says that with Him, everything is possible. And that is literally the meaning of my name (*Ife anyi Chukwu*).

And He has fulfilled His promise to me by making this book a reality. He has not only given me a book, He has taught me life, and I would forever be grateful to Him. He gave us His assurance that nothing can separate us from His love and I am holding on to that promise, because it never fails. There is nothing that comes out of the mouth of God that does not happen as He says it, because HE IS GOD, and I am glad I know Him.

I thank God for my children and the great joy they bring into my life. Their readiness to help provided me with great assistance in the writing of this book, especially Ifenna, who helped me decipher the meaning of Christianity; and Chukwunonso who helped me in the design of the cover page and in document formatting; and Chiamaka for her general encouragement, and Ifeanyi Jr for overall support and editing of the book.

My wife deserves kudos for receptively listening to hours and hours of revelations I received while writing this book, offering insights and showing support for the messages in the book, in spite of her fragile health as she recovers from a life-changing surgery.

i

Chapter 1

God Created the Earth and the Universe

Timelines, Materials, Expertise, Purpose and Activities:

On or before Genesis 1:1 God created the following in preparation for the rest of His creation project: water and the earth. These are matters and were created ahead of everything else in the entire universe.

The earth is so pivotal in creation, that throughout the Bible God always refers to 'heavens' and 'the earth' because they were each discrete and created separately and for different reasons. And the creation order was the earth before the universe—the universe is mostly referred to as heaven in the Bible.

The universe is the heaven we see, but there are other heavens, the Bible makes us understand: *"You alone are the Lord. You made the heavens, <u>even the highest heavens,</u> and all their starry host, the earth and all that is on it, the seas and all that is in them. You give life to everything, <u>and the multitudes of heaven worship you.</u>"* *(Nehemiah 9:6).*

1) **Purpose and Outcome (the intended use and what was expected):**

God established the purposes and the outcomes of the creation project before the project began. The earth, the universe, the seas, the air and various other gases, the working mechanism of everything that would result from the finished project, the intermediate products and how they were going to be used, and the other subtleties involved were all clearly thought out before the project started.

Here is why God said He created the earth—in God's own words:
"It is I who made the earth and
• *created mankind on it.*
My own hands stretched out the heavens;
I marshaled their starry hosts." (Isaiah 45:12).

"For this is what the LORD says—
he who created the heavens,
he is God;
he who fashioned and made the earth, he founded it;
he did not create it to be empty, but

• *formed it to be inhabited—*
he says:
"I am the LORD, and there is no other." (Isaiah 45:18).

And here is why God said He created the heaven (the universe) of Genesis 1:1—in God's own words:

"14 And God said, Let there be lights in the firmament of the heaven to

- *divide the day from the night; and let them be*
- *for signs, and*
- *for seasons, and*
- *for days, and*
- *years: (Genesis 1:14).*

15 And let them be

- *for lights in the firmament of the heaven*
- *to give light upon the earth: and it was so. (Genesis 1:15).*

16   And God made two great lights; the greater light to rule the day, and the lesser light to rule the night: he made the stars also.

17 And God set them in the firmament of the heaven to give light upon the earth,

18 And to rule over the day and over the night, and to divide the light from the darkness: and God saw that it was good.

19 And the evening and the morning were the fourth day." (Genesis 1:16-19).

Here is what God said—in God's own words—that caused the darkness on the earth at the very beginning *(Genesis 1:2):* **"Who shut up the sea behind doors when it burst forth from the womb, *9* when I made the clouds its garment and wrapped it in thick darkness"** *(Job 38:8-9).*

From this passage in the Book of Job, God is saying that clouds were the reason why the surface of the earth in Genesis 1:2 was in darkness. The thick dark cloud apparently arose from the dumping of huge amounts of water over the volcanic mass that was under water in Genesis 1:2. The quenching of the volcanic mass—the mass which God called the earth, which was under the deluge of water—generated such massive amount of vapor it darkened the face of the earth (that is, the earth's atmosphere).

At God's command in Genesis 1:3-5, the light appeared on the earth; and at the appearance of the light, the darkness on one half of the sphere that is the earth was overcome by the light and vanished instantly. And the other half of the sphere that is the earth remained in darkness since it had not received the light. This clearly established that the earth is spherical.

The power of the light set the **earth in rotation**—as desired by God—so that every part of the dark side of the earth would come to the light and be illuminated for a time just like the part that was hit by the light at its first appearance on the earth. This is why **"there was evening, and there was morning—the first day"** *(Genesis 1:5)*.

After the light first appeared, evening came, and morning followed to mark the conclusion of the first day and the beginning of the second day. The rotational movement of the earth started on Day 1 of God's creation, otherwise **"And there was evening and there was morning—the first day,"** would not have taken place, as recorded in Genesis 1:5. So it was:

First the light dawned → then evening came → and morning followed.

The revolution of the earth around the sun had not been established at this point since the sun had not yet been created. That is why the Genesis 1:5 simply says: **"God called the light 'day' and the darkness he called 'night.' ...,"** *(Genesis 1:5),* because those were the only two time-based events started on the first day.

This darkness that came on the earth in the form of clouds that first day, further symbolized the darkness of the heart which would ultimately descend on the earth and coexist with the light/the righteousness of God until Christ returns to defeat the darkness and stamp it out forever.

The mechanisms for the year (revolution around the sun), the seasons (positioning of the sun from the 'Tropic of Cancer' to the 'Tropic of Capricorn') and the minor light at night (the moon) were all created on Day 4; not on Day 1, indicating that the moon was more for sign than for light.

Just as the moon reflects the light from the sun, the sun, the stars, the quasi, etc., reflect the light from the 'True Light' *(John 1:9),* our Lord Jesus Christ, the Son of God of whom the Bible says: **"In the beginning was the Word, and the Word was with God, and the Word was God. He was with God in the beginning."** *(John 1:1-2)*

[3] **"Through him all things were made; without him nothing was made that has been made. [4] In him was**

life, and that life was the light of all mankind. [5] The light shines in the darkness, and the darkness has not overcome it." (John 1:3-5).

[6] "There was a man sent from God whose name was John. [7] He came as a witness to testify concerning that light, so that through him all might believe. [8] He himself was not the light; he came only as a witness to the light." (John 1:6-7).

[9] "The true light that gives light to everyone was coming into the world. [10] He was in the world, and though the world was made through him, the world did not recognize him. [11] He came to that which was his own, but his own did not receive him. [12] Yet to all who did receive him, to those who believed in his name, he gave the right to become children of God— [13] children born not of natural descent, nor of human decision or a husband's will, but born of God." (John 1:9-13).

[14] "The Word became flesh and made his dwelling among us. We have seen his glory, the glory of the one and only Son, who came from the Father, full of grace and truth." (John 1:14).

'The Word became flesh and made his dwelling among us.' This is the reality of the Jesus Christ we all know and talk about. But there is the larger picture we mostly overlook when we try to decide what Jesus Christ truly represents and who He really is. And that is that He *"In the beginning was the Word, and the Word was with God, and the Word was God. He was with God in the beginning." (John 1:1-2)*

[3] "Through him all things were made; without him nothing was made that has been made. [4] In him was life, and that life was the light of all mankind.

⁵ The light shines in the darkness, and the darkness has not overcome it." (John 1:3-5).

We must keep in mind everything the Bible says He is to fully understand and appreciate all the revelations in this book. The first thing that should spring into everybody's mind when we hear the name Jesus the Son of God must not be that He came into the world two thousand years ago; but rather that the Son is one part of the Trinity that we know as God, so He is in every way in the Father and the Father is in every way in Him:

¹⁰ "Don't you believe that I am in the Father, and that the Father is in me? The words I say to you I do not speak on my own authority. Rather, it is the Father, living in me, who is doing his work. ¹¹ <u>Believe me when I say that I am in the Father and the Father is in me</u>; or at least believe on the evidence of the works themselves." (John 14:10-11).

Let us recall that God's main objective in creating the earth was to create a habitation for His most cherished creation—the human beings: *"It is I who made the earth and created mankind on it. My own hands stretched out the heavens; I marshaled their starry hosts." (Isaiah 45:12).*

"For this is what the LORD says—he who created the heavens, he is God; he who fashioned and made the earth, he founded it; he did not create it to be empty, but formed it to be inhabited—he says: "I am the LORD, and there is no other." (Isaiah 45:18).

"Then God said, "Let us make mankind <u>in our image, in our likeness, so that they may rule</u> over the fish in the sea and the birds in the sky, over the livestock and all

the wild animals, and over all the creatures that move along the ground." (Genesis 1:26).

[27] *"So God created mankind in his own image, in the image of God he created them; male and female he created them." (Genesis 1:27).*

[28] *"God blessed them and said to them, "Be fruitful and increase in number; fill the earth and subdue it. Rule over the fish in the sea and the birds in the sky and over every living creature that moves on the ground." (Genesis 1:28).*

[29] *"Then God said, "I give you every seed-bearing plant on the face of the whole earth and every tree that has fruit with seed in it. They will be yours for food.* [30] *And to all the beasts of the earth and all the birds in the sky and all the creatures that move along the ground— everything that has the breath of life in it—I give every green plant for food." And it was so." (Genesis 1:29-30).*

[31] *"God saw all that he had made, and it was very good. And there was evening, and there was morning—the sixth day." (Genesis 1:31).*

God made the earth expressly to house mankind. And He created everything on it that mankind would need to be successful in life. He made mankind in His own image and likeness and gave mankind dominion over everything on the earth. It is important to note that God created everything on the earth and in the universe before He created mankind on the earth.

Man was His last physical creation and His most important creation; and was meant and designed to reflect the qualities of God; just as the moon reflects the light of the sun and the sun reflects the light of the True Light—Jesus Christ. We are made in the image and likeness of God so we can live and operate like God does.

And everything we need to be able to live and operate like God is built into each and every one of us. We are allowed the power to switch it on or off, and that power to choose is our will. Only our desire to honor the Father can activate the switch and turn it on. And our unwillingness to honor the Father automatically opens the door to the devil to come into our lives.

Man is never devoid of spirit—He is always controlled by the Spirit of life or the evil spirit. The one that is in control of his life at any given time is dependent on the choices he makes at any given instance in his life. The earth is our home and was equipped with every imaginable thing we need for successful lives. But the key to that home is our will which we must use the right way to gain the right access to the things God had made available to us.

2) **Know-How (expertise)** guaranteed and checked off:

a. <u>**The Creation of Matter:**</u>

God created water and the earth from nothing—and this is the origin of matter; and preceded all other creations, both on the earth and in the universe. **Matter** (water and the earth – *Genesis 1:2*) was created before time.

In essence, matter was created before time, and time was created before space and space was created before the universe, and the universe was created through the Big Bang.

Ionization from the original light—Jesus Christ—produced the earth's life-supporting gases since God created the earth to support life.

Matter → Time → Space → Universe

Order of Creation *(Genesis 1:1-19)*

b. **The creation of Time:**

The introduction of light on the earth is the beginning of **time**. God commanded for light to be on the earth and His Son Jesus Christ who ***"has life in Him, the life which is the light of men"*** *(John 1:4-5)* became the light on the earth. And the moment the light appears, time started ticking. And Day 1 was counted when evening came, and morning followed—*(Genesis 1:3-5)*.

c. **The Creation of Space:**

The stretching of the void inside water to create the expanse under vacuum is the creation of **space,** as we know it today. The whole point of carrying out the stretching of the void under water is to create vacuum inside the void as the void increased in size. The vacuum was created *(Genesis 1:6-8)* inside the expanse (space) to help propel flying objects to the farthest reaches of space in the Big Bang that followed.

d. The Creation of the universe:

At God's command, His Son Jesus Christ, who **"has life in Him, the life which is the light of men"** *(John 1:4-5)*— and who was already the light that dawned on the earth that kicked off Day 1— immensely intensified to the point of explosion, breaking up into trillions of huge flying fire balls. *(Genesis 1:14-19).* And the **universe** was born.

Through this cataclysmic explosion— the Big Bang— controlled by the Spirit of God, the sun, the stars, the quasi, the satellites, the planets, and all other celestial bodies were created and dispersed throughout space. And the Spirit of God organized them into various clusters and positioned them at various places across the space. He assigned functions and orbits to the various objects within each cluster and set them in synchronized motions, giving them speed and revolutionary directions.

He established their inter-relationships and created an awesome array of sparkling beauty across the sky to silence

His critics and inspire awe in the hearts of all mankind. *(Ephesians 4:10).*

These flying fiery objects were propelled farther and farther into space and scattered in clusters of various arrangements, and aided by the vacuum that was created within the space. They were set in place in orbits and assigned gravities by the Spirit of God, and set in motion as desired by God; to serve the goals for which God made the creation. *(Ephesians 4:4-10).*

It is important to note here that gravity is nothing other than the Spirit of God Himself. The Spirit of God was over the earth from the very first instant of creation and never lifted off *(Genesis 1:2)*. The Bible says:

*[15] The Son is the image of the invisible God, the firstborn over all creation. [16] For in him all things were created: things in heaven and on earth, visible and invisible, whether thrones or powers or rulers or authorities; all things have been created through him and for him. [17] He is before all things, **and in him all things hold together.** [18] And he is the head of the body, the church; he is the beginning and the firstborn from among the dead, so that in everything he might have the supremacy. [19] For God was pleased to have all his fullness dwell in him, [20] and through him to reconcile to himself all things, whether things on earth or things in heaven, by making peace through his blood, shed on the cross." (Colossians 1:15-20).*

"And in him all things hold together:" Jesus Christ is the glue that holds all of creation together, both on the earth and in the universe. All of the natural forces that fulfill different functions in the working of the earth, and in the working of the entire universe, are different manifestations of the Spirit of God operating through His Son, Jesus Christ, through whom God made everything and for whom God made everything.

This is further clarified and strengthened in Ephesians: *[4] "There is one body and one Spirit, just as you were called to one hope when you were called; [5] one Lord, one faith, one baptism; [6]* **one God and Father of all, who is** <u>**over all**</u> **and** <u>**through all**</u> **and** <u>**in all.**</u>*" (Ephesians 4:4-6).*

e. <u>**The creation of Land:**</u>

The land was created out of the water through controlled but expansive and violent volcanic eruptions, that created huge tsunamis and violent storms that cooled the massive land mass; encapsulating huge stretches of water in gigantic pockets within the newly formed earth to further cool the earth's crust and provide water for rivers and streams that later came to the surface of the earth to water the fields and provide clean drinking water for man and the animals, and also became reservoirs for the water God used during the time of Noah to wreck devastation on the world of that time.

f. **The creation of life of the earth**:

God had all the angles covered. Through His Son Jesus Christ, who **"has life in Him, the life which is the light of men"** *(John 1:4-5)* God created life on the earth as written in Genesis Chapter One.

Consider also the following passages:

28 "**'For in him we live and move and have our being.'** *As some of your own poets have said,* **'We are his offspring.'**" *(Acts 17:24-28)*. In essence, our lives are integral part of God because life is extended to each and every one of us from God, and continuously and inseparably connected directly to God Himself.

"By wisdom the LORD laid the earth's foundations,
by understanding he set the heavens in place;
20 **by his knowledge the watery depths were divided,**
and the clouds let drop the dew." *(Proverbs 3:19-20)*.

"For with God nothing shall be impossible." *(Luke 1:35-37)*.

3) **Budget**

The budget was established and checked off as more than adequate —materials, quality goals, utility values, etc. God was about to create everything and all He needed to create them was Himself. He is able and He is sufficient. How did I know this to be true? Look at the following passage from the gospels:

[26] *"If anyone comes to me and does not hate father and mother, wife and children, brothers and sisters—yes, even their own life—such a person cannot be my disciple.* [27] *And whoever does not carry their cross and follow me cannot be my disciple." (Luke 14:26-27).*

[28] ***"Suppose one of you wants to build a tower. Won't you first sit down and estimate the cost to see if you have enough money to complete it?*** [29] ***For if you lay the foundation and are not able to finish it, everyone who sees it will ridicule you,*** [30] ***saying, 'This person began to build and wasn't able to finish.'"*** *(Luke 14:28-30).*

[31] ***"Or suppose a king is about to go to war against another king. Won't he first sit down and consider whether he is able with ten thousand men to oppose the one coming against him with twenty thousand?*** [32] ***If he is not able, he will send a delegation while the other is still a long way off and will ask for terms of peace.*** [33] ***In the same way, those of you who do not give up everything you have cannot be my disciples."*** *(Luke 14:31-33).*

Therefore, God knew from the beginning that He had everything He needed to complete His creation project before He embarked on the creation project.

[24] *"The <u>God</u> who made the world and everything in it is the Lord of heaven and earth and <u>does not live in temples built by human hands</u>. [25] And <u>he is not served by human hands, as if he needed anything</u>. Rather, <u>he himself gives everyone life and breath and everything else</u>. [26] From one man he made all the nations, that they should inhabit the whole earth; and <u>he marked out their appointed times in history and the boundaries of their lands</u>. [27] God did this so that they would seek him and perhaps reach out for him and find him, though he is not far from any one of us. [28] 'For in him we live and move and have our being.' As some of your own poets have said, 'We are his offspring.' (Acts 17:24-28).*

[29] *"Therefore since we are God's offspring, we should not think that the divine being is like gold or silver or stone—an image made by human design and skill. [30] In the past God overlooked such ignorance, but now he commands all people everywhere to repent. [31] For he has set a day when he will judge the world with justice by the man he has appointed. He has given proof of this to everyone by raising him from the dead." (Acts 17:29-31).*

4) **Material Resources:**

    a.**Source of <u>light</u> & <u>heat</u> and <u>life</u> established**

God through His Son Jesus Christ was going to provide these resources- and would later impart light and heat onto stars, sun, quasi, etc. *(Genesis 1:14-19).*

The Light that dawned on the earth the first day—which on the fourth day was dispersed throughout the universe— produced the necessary ionization that produced all the necessary gases. And the earth, its gases and its waters were encapsulated, capped by the ionosphere and contained by its gravity.

The earth was primed for life whereas the rest of the universe was not. That explains why the earth is filled with life supporting gases that are not found elsewhere in the universe.

So any attempt by humans to start another world outside of the earth would unfailingly lead to a catastrophic ending for whatever lives humans would established in that world, because humans will not be able to sustain life there; they are not authorized to, rather, they will be doing something like that to spite God.

Life in the form of vegetation (grass, shrubs, fruit trees, non-fruit trees and other green vegetation) was created on the earth on Day 3 following the creation of land out of the water on the same Day 3—*Genesis 1:9-*

13—meaning that the earth's atmosphere (gases) had been completed to support plant growth.

The Bible says that the Spirit of God was hovering over the water. The Spirit of God encased the earth, its waters and its atmosphere before the Big Bang was set off, thereby protecting the fragile earth assembly from being incinerated. The Bible says that the Spirit of God was over the water. And the Bible does not say that at any point during creation that the Spirit of God lifted off from the water.

Therefore, it makes perfect sense to believe that the Spirit of God maintained His presence over the earth and the water throughout the creation process; and by so doing, protected the earth and everything it encased within its atmosphere. And for that reason, the earth stayed intact during the Big Bang that gave rise to the universe.

That God created plant life on the earth even before He created the Big Bang through which the universe was formed is a sign of unfathomable skill and immeasurable confidence on His part. He protected the plants and the fragile atmosphere of the earth from the explosive force whose outcome is the universe we know today! This is one engineering feat that was designed to showcase the power of God. Nothing like it would ever be imitated or duplicated; except by God at His own choosing.

Jesus Christ, the light of humanity *(John 1:4-5)*, cast enough light and radiation

on the earth from Day 1 through Day 3—
even though He packed more intensity than
that— and produced the right gases that
support life on the earth; and sealed off the
earth's atmosphere.

Then on Day 4, at God's command—
***"Let there be lights in the firmament of the
heaven to <u>divide the day from the night</u>; <u>and
let them be for signs</u>, and <u>for seasons</u>, and
<u>for days</u>, and <u>years</u>:</u>*** [15] ***And let them be for
lights in the firmament of the heaven to give
light upon the earth"*** *(Genesis 1:14-15)*—His
light increased in intensity to the point that
was necessary to light up the entire universe
and set ablaze the stars, the quasi and the
sun, so that God's purpose would be
achieved.

And about the Spirit of God, right after
He created the universe in the Big Bang
through His Son Jesus Christ, He was at
hand to create more life on the earth:
aquatic life, terrestrial life and then human
beings. The Bible says of man: ***"The Spirit of
God has made me; the breath of the Almighty
gives me life."*** *(Job 33:4)*.

b. The <u>Air</u> and all the <u>gases</u> on the earth

The air and all the gases on the earth
came from ionization energies supplied by
the original source of light from Day 1 to Day
3 (Jesus Christ). The earth's atmosphere was
completed and blocked off—protected by the

Spirit of God who was hovering over the water from the very beginning *(Genesis 1:2)*.

The Big Bang further generated more gases and the sun, the stars and the quasi continue to generate more gases in their respective orbital systems as designed by the Creator and set in motion when the Creator ascended higher than all the heavens in order to fill the whole universe: "*He who descended is the very one who ascended higher than all the heavens, in order to fill the whole universe.*" (Ephesians 4:10).

5) **Waste Containment and management— *through recycling and regeneration*:**

a. Waste management and control was planned and provided for before the project started. Organic matters recycle through decay, provides nutrition for plants, worms, microorganisms in the soil, and plants produce food for man and all the other animals.

b. Erosion contours the surface of the earth as necessary, generating topsoil and releasing minerals trapped in rocks to be utilized by plants and land-borne organisms.

c. Carbon dioxide is taken in by plants to produce Oxygen as its digestive byproduct during photosynthesis; and animals breathe in the oxygen and give off carbon dioxide as the waste from their respiration; and the cycle continues.

d. The sun heats up the earth and moisture rises into the sky, concentrates into the clouds, condenses and precipitates into rain and comes down to the earth and waters the fields and provides drinking water to animals in the wild.

e. The heat from the sun heats up the earth's atmosphere and sterilizes the air by reducing the amount of air-borne pathogens, to keep life on the earth safe and sound.

f. God established the food chain and monitors the levels of the different species to keep balance in the wild and around human beings. Consider the following passage from the Bible:

[10] *"For six years you are to sow your fields and harvest the crops,* [11] *but during the seventh year let the land lie unplowed and unused. Then the poor among your people may get food from it, and the wild animals may eat what is left. Do the same with your vineyard and your olive grove." (Exodus 23:10-11).*

[12] *"Six days do your work, but on the seventh day do not work, so that your ox and your donkey may rest, and so that the slave born in your household and the foreigner living among you may be refreshed. (Exodus 23:12).*

[27] *"I will send my terror ahead of you and throw into confusion every nation you encounter. I will make all your enemies turn their backs and run. [28] I will send the hornet ahead of you to drive the Hivites, Canaanites and Hittites out of your way. [29]* **But I will not drive them out in a single year, because the land would become desolate and the wild animals too numerous for you. [30] Little by little I will drive them out before you, until you have increased enough to take possession of the land.** *(Exodus 23:27-30).*

6) **The ability to Forever <u>maintain</u>, <u>manage</u>, <u>control</u> and <u>reinvigorate</u> what He was creating**:

God acknowledged to Himself that He has the ability to forever manage, maintain and control the earth and the universe before He sets out create them. God made sure to permeate everything He created and be the glue that holds each piece together and the glue that holds all together in perfect harmony, function and esthetics. Look at the following passage from the Bible:

"Listen to me, Jacob, Israel, whom I have called: I am he; <u>I am the first and am the last.</u> [13] My own hand laid the foundations of the earth, and my right hand spread out the heavens; <u>when I summon them, they all stand up together."</u> *(Isaiah48:12-13).*

God knew it would all come together the way it all did. That was His intent and He knew from the very onset that He could pull it all off. And He also knew that ironically man would misunderstand and misuse His handiwork.

That is why God made the vapor that arose from the cooling of the earth to concentrate and cast darkness across the entire surface of the earth. And God had His Spirit hovering over the water, to contain both the earth and the darkness, signifying that He will always be triumphant over everything. His confidence in doing as He wishes is evident in all His warnings to man throughout the Bible. Here are some:

[18] "If after all this you will not listen to me, I will punish you for your sins seven times over. [19] I will break down your stubborn pride and make the sky above you like iron and the ground beneath you like bronze. [20] Your strength will be spent in vain, because your soil will not yield its crops, nor will the trees of your land yield their fruit." (Leviticus 26:18-20).

[21] "If you remain hostile toward me and refuse to listen to me, I will multiply your afflictions seven times over, as your sins deserve. [22] I will send wild animals against you, and they will rob you of your children, destroy your cattle and make you so few in number that your roads will be deserted." (Leviticus 26:21-22).

[23] "'If in spite of these things you do not accept my correction but continue to be hostile toward me, [24] I myself will be hostile toward you and will afflict you for your sins seven times over. [25] And I will bring the sword on you to avenge the breaking of

the covenant. When you withdraw into your cities, I will send a plague among you, and you will be given into enemy hands. ²⁶ When I cut off your supply of bread, ten women will be able to bake your bread in one oven, and they will dole out the bread by weight. You will eat, but you will not be satisfied." (Leviticus 26:23-26).

²⁷ "'If in spite of this you still do not listen to me but continue to be hostile toward me, ²⁸ then in my anger I will be hostile toward you, and I myself will punish you for your sins seven times over. ²⁹ You will eat the flesh of your sons and the flesh of your daughters. ³⁰ I will destroy your high places, cut down your incense altars and pile your dead bodies[b] on the lifeless forms of your idols, and I will abhor you. ³¹ I will turn your cities into ruins and lay waste your sanctuaries, and I will take no delight in the pleasing aroma of your offerings. ³² I myself will lay waste the land, so that your enemies who live there will be appalled. ³³ I will scatter you among the nations and will draw out my sword and pursue you. Your land will be laid waste, and your cities will lie in ruins. ³⁴ Then the land will enjoy its sabbath years all the time that it lies desolate and you are in the country of your enemies; then the land will rest and enjoy its sabbaths. ³⁵ All the time that it lies desolate, the land will have the rest it did not have during the sabbaths you lived in it." (Leviticus 26:27-35).

"Call if you will, but who will answer you?
    To which of the holy ones will you turn?
² Resentment kills a fool,
    and envy slays the simple.
³ I myself have seen a fool taking root,
    but suddenly his house was cursed.
⁴ His children are far from safety,
    crushed in court without a defender.

⁵ The hungry consume his harvest,
  taking it even from among thorns,
  and the thirsty pant after his wealth.
⁶ For hardship does not spring from the soil,
  nor does trouble sprout from the ground.
⁷ Yet man is born to trouble
  as surely as sparks fly upward." (Job 5:1-7).

⁸ "But if I were you, I would appeal to God;
  I would lay my cause before him.
⁹ He performs wonders that cannot be fathomed,
  miracles that cannot be counted.
¹⁰ He provides rain for the earth;
  he sends water on the countryside.
¹¹ The lowly he sets on high,
  and those who mourn are lifted to safety.
¹² He thwarts the plans of the crafty,
  so that their hands achieve no success.
¹³ He catches the wise in their craftiness,
  and the schemes of the wily are swept away.
¹⁴ Darkness comes upon them in the daytime;
  at noon they grope as in the night.
¹⁵ He saves the needy from the sword in their mouth;
  he saves them from the clutches of the powerful.
¹⁶ So the poor have hope,
  and injustice shuts its mouth." (Job 5:8-16).

¹⁷ "Blessed is the one whom God corrects;
  so do not despise the discipline of the Almighty.
¹⁸ For he wounds, but he also binds up;
  he injures, but his hands also heal.
¹⁹ From six calamities he will rescue you;
  in seven no harm will touch you.
²⁰ In famine he will deliver you from death,
  and in battle from the stroke of the sword.
²¹ You will be protected from the lash of the tongue,
  and need not fear when destruction comes.
²² You will laugh at destruction and famine,

and need not fear the wild animals.
23 For you will have a covenant with the stones of the field,
    and the wild animals will be at peace with you.
24 You will know that your tent is secure;
    you will take stock of your property and find nothing missing.
25 You will know that your children will be many,
    and your descendants like the grass of the earth.
26 You will come to the grave in full vigor,
    like sheaves gathered in season." (Job 5:17-26).

27 "We have examined this, and it is true.
    So hear it and apply it to yourself." (Job 5:27).

"During the reign of David, there was a famine for three successive years; so David sought the face of the LORD. The LORD said, "It is on account of Saul and his blood-stained house; it is because he put the Gibeonites to death." *(2 Samuel 21:1).*

2 The king summoned the Gibeonites and spoke to them. (Now the Gibeonites were not a part of Israel but were survivors of the Amorites; the Israelites had sworn to spare them, but Saul in his zeal for Israel and Judah had tried to annihilate them.) 3 David asked the Gibeonites, "What shall I do for you? How shall I make atonement so that you will bless the LORD's inheritance?" *(2 Samuel 21:2-3).*

4 The Gibeonites answered him, "We have no right to demand silver or gold from Saul or his family, nor do we have the right to put anyone in Israel to death."

"What do you want me to do for you?" David asked. *(2 Samuel 21:4).*

⁵ They answered the king, "As for the man who destroyed us and plotted against us so that we have been decimated and have no place anywhere in Israel, ⁶ let seven of his male descendants be given to us to be killed and their bodies exposed before the L<small>ORD</small> at Gibeah of Saul—the L<small>ORD</small>'s chosen one."

So the king said, "I will give them to you." (2 Samuel 21:5-6).

⁷ The king spared Mephibosheth son of Jonathan, the son of Saul, because of the oath before the L<small>ORD</small> between David and Jonathan son of Saul. ⁸ But the king took Armoni and Mephibosheth, the two sons of Aiah's daughter Rizpah, whom she had borne to Saul, together with the five sons of Saul's daughter Merab, whom she had borne to Adriel son of Barzillai the Meholathite. ⁹ He handed them over to the Gibeonites, who killed them and exposed their bodies on a hill before the L<small>ORD</small>. All seven of them fell together; they were put to death during the first days of the harvest, just as the barley harvest was beginning." (2 Samuel 21:7-9).

¹⁰ Rizpah daughter of Aiah took sackcloth and spread it out for herself on a rock. From the beginning of the harvest till the rain poured down from the heavens on the bodies, she did not let the birds touch them by day or the wild animals by night. ¹¹ When David was told what Aiah's daughter Rizpah, Saul's concubine, had done, ¹² he went and took the bones of Saul and his son Jonathan from the citizens of Jabesh Gilead. (They had stolen their bodies from the public square at Beth Shan, where the Philistines had hung them after they struck Saul down on Gilboa.) ¹³ David brought the bones of Saul and his son Jonathan from there, and the bones of those who had been killed and exposed were gathered up." (2 Samuel 21:10-13).

¹⁴ They buried the bones of Saul and his son Jonathan in the tomb of Saul's father Kish, at Zela in Benjamin, and did everything the king commanded. <u>After that, God answered prayer in behalf of the land</u>. *(2 Samuel 21:14).*

"This is what the Lord Almighty, the God of Israel, says: I will put an iron yoke on the necks of all these nations to make them serve Nebuchadnezzar king of Babylon, and they will serve him. I will even give him control over the wild animals.'" (Jeremiah 28:14).

"This is what the Lord Almighty, the God of Israel, says: I will put an iron yoke on the necks of all these nations to make them serve Nebuchadnezzar king of Babylon, and they will serve him. I will even give him control over the wild animals.'" *(Ezekiel 14:21).*

"You will be driven away from people and will live with **the wild animals**; you will eat grass like **the** ox and be drenched with **the** dew of heaven. Seven times will pass by for you until you acknowledge that **the** Most High is sovereign over all kingdoms on earth and gives **the**m to anyone he wishes." (Daniel 4:25).

There are countless other passages throughout the Bible that demonstrate God's confidence and His effective management and control of the earth and everything in it. Let me use this opportunity to remind the reader that the spirit in every man, woman and child on the earth is 'God in us' (Ephesians 4:4-6). As such, Jesus Christ is every cell in our bodies and directs every aspect of our lives. Christ is also in every atom in everything on the earth and in the universe (Ephesians 4:10) and (Genesis 1:14-19). And this is the grand purpose of creation!

7) **Project Timeframe established**:

God allowed Himself only six days to complete the entire creation project *(Genesis 1:1-31)*. He made the earth, time, the seas, space and the universe together with all the celestial bodies; all arranged in galaxies, all set in orbits and functions as designed. And in only six days He got the whole job done.

8) **Labor and manpower**:

God reckoned His own ability to do all things alone and yet efficiently. He checked that off. The following is an itemization of some of God's qualities that made it possible for Him to single-handedly create the earth and the universe:

a.**Being the Spirit:**
  i. **"_God is spirit_, and his worshipers must worship in the Spirit and in truth."** *(John 4:24)*. And because God is spirit, all-powerful, all-knowing and all-discerning, He knows everything and could get into any situation anytime and accomplish whatever He sets His mind on. He and He alone could get the whole job done in a short amount of time and He did it in only six days.

b. **Having Mighty Right Hand** *(Psalms 77:15)*:

i.   Enables Him to put actions behind His thoughts and execute His plans successfully: **"My own <u>hand</u> laid the foundations of the earth, and my <u>right hand</u> spread out the heavens; when I summon them, they all stand up together."** (Isaiah 48:13).

ii.   Allows Him to protect all the things He had created and guarantee their safety.

iii. Allows Him to deal decisively with the wicked and trouble makers whose main purpose in life is to seek glory for themselves ahead of giving glory to God.

iv.   Allows Him to stir up the sea, the wind, the earth and the celestial bodies to demonstrate His capability to mankind and warn and rebuke mankind when they get out of line.

c. Having an unfathomably Huge Mind:

i.   Allows Him to think only beautiful thoughts

ii.   Allows Him to come up with the grandest designs.

iii. Helps Him keeps count of the where-about of all mankind and the heavenly hosts and continue to order and direct their every steps.

iv. Allows Him to maintain meticulous records of everything that takes place in His universe, including who does what to who and who does good and who does evil, and intervene whenever He think necessary to intervene.

d. Having infinite Love *(Psalms 77:7-12):*

i. Puts all the celestial bodies in space into perpetual motions that together mesmerize and sing lullaby to His children on the earth, and continue to entertain the heavenly hosts.

ii. Allows Him to be longsuffering and continue to forgive and have mercy on mankind even when mankind deliberately berate Him and disrespect Him.

iii. Makes Him faithful to mankind to bring mankind back into His eternal purpose and even sacrificed the life of His begotten Son to achieve that.

iv. Makes Him give His favors to mankind even when mankind is underserving of His consideration.

e. Having a supernatural and eternal body:

i. Gives Him the ability to go in and out of everything and anything without the need for an egress.

ii. Gives Him the ability to assume the right form (solid, liquid, gas), size and shape for the right occasion and the right job.

iii. Gives Him the ability to adapt His energy into various forms at the right time and the right circumstance—even into many different forms in any given time.

iv. Gives Him the ability to have all kinds of different natural effects (ionization levels as in electromagnetic spectrum, etc.— radio one moment, gamma the next, and everything else in between at various other points); and supernatural effects (spiritual renewal, spiritual healing, etc.) on anything at an instant and change it over in a split of a second.

v. Gives Him the ability to be all of the above, and all at once, in trillions of places at the same time—as in the final showcase He left for mankind in the form of our current universe. What a marvel?

f. Having the ability to create whatever technique He needed to perform any function:

God has the ability to do whatever He chooses to do, including separation of even the inseparable. Here is a passage to consider: **"For the word of God is alive and active. Sharper than any double-edged sword, it penetrates even to dividing soul and spirit, joints and marrow; it judges the thoughts and attitudes of the heart. [13] Nothing in all creation is hidden from God's sight. Everything is uncovered and laid bare before the eyes of him to whom we must give account."** *(Hebrews 4:12-13).*

The separation of soul from the spirit is the most intricate separation and no one but God can do this. We do not even know what the soul looks like or what the human spirit looks like. We do not even know what the two of them combined looks like, how then can we even attempt to separate them? If God is able to separate the soul from the spirit, then He is capable of separating heat from cold and everything and anything.

In the natural, separation of heat from cold could prove useful in erecting standing walls of water on all sides of 'the void inside the water' in *Genesis 1:6-8*. With sliding walls of ice lining the void, the walls can be pushed or pulled out to enlarge the void and increase the size of it as well as the vacuum inside the void.

But God operates in the supernatural and does everything and anything to His heart's delight. Therefore, creating space was no challenge at all to God. The Bible says: *"For with God nothing shall be impossible." (Luke 1:35-37).*

When Moses led the Israelites through the red sea, the Bible says: *"Then Moses stretched out his hand over the sea, and <u>all that night the LORD drove the sea back with a strong east wind and turned it into dry land</u>. <u>The waters were divided,</u> ²² and the Israelites went through the sea on dry ground, <u>with a wall of water on their right and on their left</u>." (Exodus 14:21-22).*

If God was able to on-demand cause the Red Sea to part and leave dry grounds for the Israelites to cross on, He certainly was capable of easily creating space within water in the beginning. At the Red Sea crossing which took place in the more modern time, God parted the sea overnight and dried up the water— *"all that night the LORD drove the sea back with a strong east wind and turned it into dry land." (Exodus 14:21).*

"with a wall of water on their right and on their left." (Exodus 14:22): What was keeping the water from flowing back from the walls? Can mankind explain the force

that was keeping liquid water erected into walls? Can our scientists explain the force that was keeping the walls of liquid water from flowing back into the dry grounds in the waterbed of the deep Red Sea?

Or will man's best attempt at deciphering the events be to deny that the events ever happened, even though the event was well documented? Check out the following passage: *"O my people , hear my teaching; listen to the words of my mouth. I will open my mouth in parables, I will utter hidden things, things from of old—* **what _we have heard_ and _known,_ what our fathers have told us..."** *(Psalm 78:1-72).*

Mankind so readily accepts recorded history from ancient cultures that lived well before the Red Sea parting and the other events recorded in the Bible. And we discuss everything in those accounts as if they were God-given truth. We teach them in school and grades students on how well they remember them. We model our institutions after theirs in exaltation of them and celebration of their contributions to civilization.

But when the record has to do with God and His supernatural powers, our first reacting is to question whether the documented event ever happened at all; because accepting that the event occurred would automatically force us to admit that God did everything He said that He did in the

Bible.

And once we make this admission, we lose the freedom to peddle our unfounded theories and mesmerize the world with them; thereby allowing us to continue to rake in fame and fortune, and lord it over everybody else, especially those who are less gullible to our many theories and magic.

We treat every God-given truth as a lie—a product of somebody's overactive imagination; and taking the Bible as a whole—as well-synchronized products of more than one hundred and fifty kings', prophets' and apostles' overactive minds, even though these people—kings, prophets and apostles—lived in different cultures and different times spanning more than One thousand five hundred (1500) years.

And although our current civilization was essentially built on the events recorded in the Bible, we act as though the Bible has no relevance to the lives of the modern man; as if it was a concoction of scheming and conspiring men intent on turning civilization upside down. We systematically remove everything God and Bible from our public discussions and tout science as man's last hope for survival.

Anybody who does not know how the western civilization came to be should read the following book: "HOW THE CATHOLIC CHURCH BUILT WESTERN CIVILIZATION By

Thomas E. Woods, Jr., Ph.D." Even those who know will still benefit from reading this and other books dealing with the subject of science and the church.

It is a must for every Christian or you will be caught unawares and unprepared at the return of Jesus Christ to the earth. Jesus Christ warns mankind to be ready, and this is how *(Luke 17:1-37): Be Ready!*

For your convenience this chapter of the gospel of Luke (Luke 17:1-37) is placed as an excerpt after the last chapter of this book.

The church nurtured science from its infancy into full bloom. Science eventually separated itself from the church and grew increasingly antagonistic to the church. But prophesies about these events were given to us by God through John the revelator.

The consensus among the scientists and the politicians always seems to be: It is best to keep God out of it, and move the arguments into arenas that would automatically permit only a handful of participants to shape these ideas, package them, and feed them to the rest of the world in the most profitable formats approved by the elites of the human society.

Society is really not looking for the truth of God. Society is looking whatever form of the truth that provides the maximum amount of for material gain, even if that form of truth goes against God Himself. And to be successful in this, society requires that God be put on the shelf when issues are being discussed for public interest. That way it will be purely on economic grounds.

And society retains the rights to dictate when spiritual issues could be discussed anywhere within its boundaries. Therefore society would never be right with God, because God must never be relegated to a small portion of our lives; God must be in all parts of our lives. And anybody who believes that society will provide him or her with the right guide to spiritual fulfillment is already on a path of spiritual ruin.

And this is what God says to the world systems:

⁶ I was angry with my people
and desecrated my inheritance;
I gave them into your hand,
and you showed them no mercy.
Even on the aged
you laid a very heavy yoke.
⁷ You said, 'I am forever—
the eternal queen!'
But you did not consider these things
or reflect on what might happen." (Isaiah 47:6-7)

⁸ "Now then, listen, you lover of pleasure,
lounging in your security
and saying to yourself,
'I am, and there is none besides me.
I will never be a widow

or suffer the loss of children.'
⁹ Both of these will overtake you
in a moment, on a single day:
loss of children and widowhood.
They will come upon you in full measure,
in spite of your many sorceries
and all your potent spells." *(Isaiah 47:8-9)*

¹⁰ You have trusted in your wickedness
and have said, 'No one sees me.'
Your wisdom and knowledge mislead you
when you say to yourself,
'I am, and there is none besides me.'
(Isaiah 47:10)
¹¹ Disaster will come upon you,
and you will not know how to conjure it
away.
A calamity will fall upon you
that you cannot ward off with a ransom;
a catastrophe you cannot foresee
will suddenly come upon you." *(Isaiah*
47:11)

¹² "Keep on, then, with your magic spells
and with your many sorceries,
which you have labored at since childhood.
Perhaps you will succeed,
perhaps you will cause terror." *(Isaiah*
47:12)

The Bible also says that God is fire—
²⁹ _for our "God is a consuming fire._" *(Hebrews*
12:14-29). So we know how readily He
created the volcanic mass that was under
the water in *Genesis 1:2* and all the fiery
celestial bodies that He created and
distributed throughout space to make the

universe.

"Fire came out from the presence of the Lord and consumed the burnt offering and the fat portions on the altar. And when all the people saw it, they shouted for joy and fell facedown." (Leviticus 9:24).

"Aaron's sons Nadab and Abihu took their censers, put fire in them and added incense; and they offered unauthorized fire before the LORD, contrary to his command. [2] So fire came out from the presence of the LORD and consumed them, and they died before the LORD. [3] Moses then said to Aaron, "This is what the LORD spoke of when he said:

'Among those who approach me I will be proved holy; in the sight of all the people I will be honored.' Aaron remained silent." (Leviticus 10:1-3).

"As I looked, "thrones were set in place, and the Ancient of Days took his seat. His clothing was as white as snow; the hair of his head was white like wool. His throne was flaming with fire, and its wheels were all ablaze." (Daniel 7:9).

"When Moses came down from Mount Sinai with the two tablets of the covenant law in his hands, he was not aware that his face was radiant because he had spoken with the LORD. [30] When Aaron and all the Israelites saw Moses, his face was radiant, and they were afraid to come near him. [31] But Moses called to them; so Aaron and all the leaders of the community came back to him, and he

spoke to them. ³² Afterward all the Israelites came near him, and he gave them all the commands the LORD had given him on Mount Sinai." (Exodus 34:29-33).

³³ "When Moses finished speaking to them, he put a veil over his face. ³⁴ But whenever he entered the LORD's presence to speak with him, he removed the veil until he came out. And when he came out and told the Israelites what he had been commanded, ³⁵ they saw that his face was radiant. Then Moses would put the veil back over his face until he went in to speak with the LORD." (Exodus 34:33-35).

"After six days Jesus took with him Peter, James and John the brother of James, and led them up a high mountain by themselves. ² There he was transfigured before them. His face shone like the sun, and his clothes became as white as the light. ³ Just then there appeared before them Moses and Elijah, talking with Jesus." (Matthew 17:1-3).

The Bible says*: "God made the expanse and separated the water under the vault from the water above it. And it was so." (Genesis 1:7).* And God says: *"My own hands stretched out the heavens ....," (Isaiah 45:12),* hinting that the expanse was simply stretched to enlarge it; and this stretching was done inside water. Therefore, if it was stretched inside water and water was prevented from going into it—which obviously was the case here—the water would simply form a tight seal around the expanse that not even gas would enter the expanse from outside the water.

So the expanse would remain under vacuum. And this vacuum would prove extremely useful in the energy dispersion that took place in the next step of the creation process—the Big Bang (Genesis 1:14-19). The vacuum would pull the flying balls of flame farther and farther away from the earth at the center of this expanse thereby helping to more quickly achieve the distribution objectives and cluster formations and operations intended by God.

Continuing to put these things in relatable human terms is not so we can determine whether or not God did what He says He did. It actually belittles God if our goal is to judge the feasibility of what God recorded that He did; because we do not even have the right mental capacity to understand God's complex physics, chemistry, geology and biology, let alone the ability to affirm that what He recorded in the Bible concerning His mindboggling engineering masterpiece is practical. So pardon me if that appears to be what I was doing. However, I can assure you that it is not my intent. The Bible says that the foolishness God is better than our wisdom:

[20] *"Where is the wise person? Where is the teacher of the law? Where is the philosopher of this age? Has not God made foolish the wisdom of the world?* [21] *For since in the wisdom of God the world through its wisdom did not know him, God was pleased through the foolishness of what was preached to save those who believe.* [22] *Jews demand signs*

and Greeks look for wisdom, [23] *but we preach Christ crucified: a stumbling block to Jews and foolishness to Gentiles,* [24] *but to those whom God has called, both Jews and Greeks, Christ the power of God and the wisdom of God.* [25] ***For the foolishness of God is wiser than human wisdom, and the weakness of God is stronger than human strength." (1 Corinthians 1:20-25).***

What I hope people will get out of this revelation is that God indeed left, for mankind in Genesis Chapter One, a blueprint of sophisticated and advanced science and engineering which He employed in creating the timeless marvels that are men, the earth, and the universe and everything inside them.

The world's elite scientists had actually misguided the world by reversing the order of things as God created them, making us belief that the blueprint which God left for us was a forgery and amounts to nothing; when in reality, it was their minds that were distorted because God set them on a wild goose chase so He could reveal the inferiority of their wisdom in comparison with God's wisdom.

Earth under water *(Genesis 1:2)*—water was already created and the massive blob God called the earth was already created, hot and malleable— ***"The earth takes shape like clay under a seal; its features stand out like those of a garment.*** *(Job 38:14).* God referred to this 'blob' as 'the earth' in Genesis 1:2 to establish that the earth preceded the universe and everything else in the universe.

God made that clear by giving this narrative with the very day associated with each creation so that no one would be in doubt as to what was created before what. The earth under water was the only starting raw material mentioned as present even before Day 1 dawned. But man in his 'super wisdom' decided to disregard God's own recorded timeline of the events of creation and established his own fictitious timeline that got man chasing after hot air for centuries now, in his attempt to correct God.

God clearly says in the Bible that the earth pre-dated time itself. According to God, the earth and water were created before God commanded for light on the earth for the first time in Genesis 1:3-5. Time did not start until light appeared on the earth. From that point forward, time started ticking; and **"God called the light "day," and the darkness he called "night." And there was evening, and there was morning—the first day."** (Genesis 1:5).

Therefore the earth and water predated both time and space. If God who created the earth, water, time, space and the universe clearly delineated the order in which He created these things, who is man to question the accuracy of God's account of the projects God Himself conceived, planned, designed and executed with unrivalled finesse?

On what authority is man questioning God's credibility even to the point of dismissing God's existence completely and seeking to give himself credit for simply coming up with some explanation for what was done before time began? Anyone who ignores God's truth and chases after the wind should look at the following passage again:

"The fear of the LORD is the beginning of wisdom,
 and knowledge of the Holy One is understanding.
[11] For through wisdom your days will be many,

and years will be added to your life.
¹² If you are wise, your wisdom will reward you;
    if you are a mocker, you alone will suffer." *(Proverbs 9:10-12).*

²⁸ "For in him we live and move and have our being." *(Acts 17:28).*

"Where there is no revelation, people cast off restraint; but blessed is the one who heeds wisdom's instruction." *(Proverbs 29:18).*

"From the mouth of the righteous comes the fruit of wisdom, but a perverse tongue will be silenced. The lips of the righteous know what finds favor, but the mouth of the wicked only what is perverse." *(Proverbs 9:10-31-32).*

¹⁸ For the message of the cross is foolishness to those who are perishing, but to us who are being saved it is the power of God. ¹⁹ For it is written:

"I will destroy the wisdom of the wise;
    the intelligence of the intelligent I will frustrate."[c] *(1 Corinthians 1:18-19).*

²⁰ Where is the wise person? Where is the teacher of the law? Where is the philosopher of this age? Has not God made foolish the wisdom of the world? ²¹ For since in the wisdom of God the world through its wisdom did not know him, God was pleased through the foolishness of

47

what was preached to save those who believe. [22] *Jews demand signs and Greeks look for wisdom,* [23] *but we preach Christ crucified: a stumbling block to Jews and foolishness to Gentiles,* [24] *but to those whom God has called, both Jews and Greeks, Christ the power of God and the wisdom of God.* [25] *For the foolishness of God is wiser than human wisdom, and the weakness of God is stronger than human strength.*" *(1 Corinthians 1:20-25).*

It is interesting to know that all these creation activities were not carried out in secret: God recorded in the Book of Job that all the heavenly hosts were not only witnesses to the whole creation but that they were also singing and shouting for joy. That is probably the greatest assembly the earth had ever seen and we were not around to witness it. Imagine the exhilaration and joy as they shouted together! Here is the passage from the Book of Job:

"Where were you when I laid the earth's foundation?
  Tell me, if you understand.
[5] *Who marked off its dimensions? Surely you know!*
  Who stretched a measuring line across it?
[6] *On what were its footings set,*
  or who laid its cornerstone—
[7] *while the morning stars <u>sang</u> together*
  and all the angels <u>shouted</u> for joy?" *(Job 38:4-7).*

In light of the revelation that God created the earth and the universe through His son Jesus Christ *(John 1:1-18)*; and that Jesus Christ is the true light of creation *(Genesis 1:1-5)* and the energy that was dispersed throughout the universe in the Big Bang and more *(Genesis 1:6-8)* and *(Genesis 1:14-19)*—and **Jesus Christ "ascended higher than all the heavens <u>in order to fill the whole universe</u>.**" *(Ephesians 4:6).* And that **He "is <u>over</u> all, <u>through</u> all and <u>in</u> all.**" *(Ephesians 4:10)*—which puts Him in every atom of everything in the universe; it suffices then to conclude the following (an excerpt from one of my previous books):

God is infinite energy plus the sum total of all the energies that exist in the universe, visible and invisible; thermal, nuclear, sonic, light, magnetic, electrical, chemical, potential, hydrostatic, and all of the other forms of energy known and unknown. And all this is summarized in an elementary equation as:

$$E_{God} = E^{\infty} + \sum_{n=1}^{\infty} E_n$$

Where:

E_{God} = God's Energy;

E^{∞} = Infinite Energy;

E_n = Total Energy of its kind in the universe;

n = number of energy types available in the universe, known and unknown; visible and invisible.

Jesus Christ "ascended higher than all the heavens <u>in order to fill the whole universe.</u>" (Ephesians 4:6). He "is <u>over</u> all, <u>through</u> all and <u>in</u> all." (Ephesians 4:10).

In essence, it is His presence in all things He created that gives them their forms and functions; their energy, vitality and life (in the case of living things); and their utility and interconnectedness to one another. Jesus Christ came to the earth for all; to give eternal life to the entire mankind and to make their lives on earth more abundant.

God did not make everything and at the end of the sixth day walk away. He continues to operate within all things to maintain the cohesiveness and harmony He intended to achieve when He created everything. And for those who look at the account of creation in the Book of Genesis and doubt that God did what He said He did, you have not read the rest of the Bible, so you do not and cannot understand what God is saying in Genesis. You are welcome to study the Bible. It is God's gift to all humanity.

God created us and gave us great intelligence: He made us in His own image. So being as bright as we are, is not a feat we accomplished on our own; it is something that was given to us by God. The Bible says: "But to each one of us grace has been given as Christ apportioned it. This is why it says: 'When he ascended on high, he led captives in his train and gave gifts to men.'" (Ephesians 4:7-8).

None of us was responsible for how much of that intelligence we received. It was all decided by God. He gave to each of us as He deemed necessary, not for us to become prideful but for the benefit of all humanity. That is why the Bible says: "Each one should use whatever gift he has received to serve others, faithfully administering God's grace in its various forms." (1 Peter 4:10). And it also says: "Now to each one the manifestation of the Spirit is given for the common good." (1 Corinthians 12:7).

God has no interest in justifying anything to anyone. He owes nothing to anyone. Rather, humanity owes Him for the elevated position we enjoy among all creation. The only demand God makes from any of us is faith. And if you cannot afford to give that much respect to Him, you have yourself to blame. Not only did humanity turn its back on God when Adam and Eve decided to disobey a simple command of God, we have continued to multiply the insult in so many different ways, including questioning the veracity of the things He said to us in the Bible.

Yet, out of His immense love for humanity, He sent His Son to suffer and pay for our sins; to redeem us and make us holy again, so we would be able to enter God's presence, which we have never truly known. This is a gift for all. Nobody needs to do anything to qualify for it. The only thing He requested from anybody to receive this gift is faith.

The faith we need to be cleansed of our sins and become acceptable to God is the same faith that we need to understand anything that comes out of the mouth of God. To understand the truth about anything in the universe, without assumptions and needless extrapolations, we need to have faith in God, and earnestly search the Scriptures for the truth about our world and the universe, at large.

And without faith, all our efforts continue to be a struggle — a matter of trial and error. We have done things that way throughout our history and we have not learned anything from our difficulties. The truth is glaring into everyone's face, and with the collective knowledge that exists in the world today, we could accelerate much faster in our understanding of the universe, with the added benefit of the forgiveness of our sins and the opportunity for eternal life.

When, with faith in God, you study the Bible, a new window of understanding is opened up to you. This new understanding completes and amplifies the understanding you already have in whatever specialty you are in. And things that never made sense to you before will begin to unfold right before your eyes. This is the revelation that is promised to anyone that has faith in God.

God does not discriminate. To knowledge, He adds knowledge. To wisdom, He adds wisdom. To understanding, He adds understanding. To hard work, He adds results. To humility, He adds greatness. To obedience, He adds honor and to faithfulness, He adds favor. Whatever you bring with you to the Bible, He refocuses and amplifies by the time you leave.

The opposite is also true of the Bible. If you come to the Bible with the intention of vilifying God, you will end up decimated and desecrated. Nobody can pick up a fight with God and succeed. If you came with doubts, that is a different thing. It is okay to have questions. And if you have questions and come with an open mind, you will satisfy your questions and more before you leave. God allows doubters to survive so they may have time to change their minds and gain the necessary knowledge they need to become enlightened.

To understand what God is telling you in Genesis about the creation of the universe and everything in it, you need to read the rest of the Bible in faith and in humility. The Bible is not just another book. It is the word of the all-powerful God of the universe, who does not play around but does everything with purpose. When you open the Bible, you are approaching the God that is the sum total of all the powers that exist in the universe and more. So you should approach reverently with thoughtfulness and eagerness to learn. That you are able to learn anything and retain it is Him.

The following passage from the Epistle of Peter testifies to the patience and love of God: "But do not forget this one thing, dear friends: <u>With the Lord a day is like a thousand years, and a thousand years are like a day.</u> The Lord is not slow in keeping his promise, as some understand slowness. He is patient with you, <u>not wanting anyone to perish</u>, but everyone to come to repentance." (2 Peter 3:8-9). It also demonstrates that the Almighty God, who is above time and space, looks at everything whatever way He chooses. He does not count like we do because He is not constrained by the things we are constrained by.

So when you look at the timeline in Genesis and try to determine whether to believe God's account of the creation or reject it in light of current scientific projections, you will not only hamper yourself from gaining true understanding of things, you will also hurt your chance of salvation. To understand what God is saying to you as you read the Bible, you have to abandon your constrained methods of testing knowledge, and allow the Holy Spirit of God to take you through the information and reveal the hidden secrets to you.

Remember, God has put a spirit in you, which extends

from His Spirit. When you allow your spirit to guide you as you delve into the deluge of God's wisdom that is the Bible, you emerge glistening with radiance and depth; having an understanding that negates everything else you have learned in your entire life. True knowledge comes from God, and He gives it to those who truly seek it.

The most important thing to remember is that the Bible was not given to us primarily to extend our knowledge of the universe; but to help us develop faith in God through His Son Jesus Christ, in whom are hidden all the treasures of wisdom and knowledge. Once you develop that faith, God, then, opens your eyes so you may see anything else you are looking for in the Bible. No matter what your situations or circumstances are, you can find the answers in the Bible. God is still speaking to anyone who would listen." *(Jesus On: We all live because He Lives! By Ifeanyi Chukwujama).*

Chapter 2

Here Is God Himself Telling the Story of Creation

Everything below presented in this chapter are passages of the Bible in which God or His prophets and apostles discuss how God created the earth and the universe:

"In the beginning was the Word, and the Word was with God, and the Word was God. ² He was with God in the beginning. ³ Through him all things were made; without him nothing was made that has been made. ⁴ In him was life, and that life was the light of all mankind. ⁵ The light shines in the darkness, and the darkness has not overcome[a] it. ⁶ There was a man sent from God whose name was John. ⁷ He came as a witness to testify concerning that light, so that through him all might believe. ⁸ He himself was not the light; he came only as a witness to the light." (John 1:1-8).*

⁹ The true light that gives light to everyone was coming into the world. ¹⁰ He was in the world, and though the world was made through him, the world did not recognize him. ¹¹ He came to that which was his own, but his own did not receive him. ¹² Yet to all who did receive him, to those who believed in his name, he gave the right to become children of God— ¹³ children born not of natural descent, nor of human decision or a husband's will, but born of God. [14] The Word became flesh and made his dwelling among us. We have seen his glory, the glory of the one and only Son, who came from the Father, full of grace and truth." (John 1:9-14).

[15] (John testified concerning him. He cried out, saying, "This is the one I spoke about when I said, 'He who comes after me has surpassed me because he was before me.'") [16] Out of his fullness we have all received grace in place of grace already given. [17] For the law was given through Moses; grace and truth came through Jesus Christ. [18] No one has ever seen God, but the one and only Son, who is himself God and is in closest relationship with the Father, has made him known." (John 1:15-18).

In the Book of GENESIS:

"In the beginning God created the heavens and the earth. [2] Now the earth was formless and empty, darkness was over the surface of the deep, and the Spirit of God was hovering over the waters." (Genesis 1:1-2).

[3] "And God said, "Let there be light," and there was light. [4] God saw that the light was good, and he separated the light from the darkness. [5] God called the light "day," and the darkness he called "night." And there was evening, and there was morning—the first day." (Genesis 3-5).

[6] "And God said, "Let there be a vault between the waters to separate water from water." [7] So God made the vault and separated the water under the vault from the water above it. And it was so. [8] God called the vault "sky." And there was evening, and there was morning—the second day." (Genesis 6-8).

9 "And God said, "Let the water under the sky be gathered to one place, and let dry ground appear." And it was so. 10 God called the dry ground "land," and the gathered waters he called "seas." And God saw that it was good. (Genesis 9-10).

11 "Then God said, "Let the land produce vegetation: seed-bearing plants and trees on the land that bear fruit with seed in it, according to their various kinds." And it was so. 12 The land produced vegetation: plants bearing seed according to their kinds and trees bearing fruit with seed in it according to their kinds. And God saw that it was good. 13 And there was evening, and there was morning— the third day." (Genesis 1:11-13).

14 "And God said, "Let there be lights in the vault of the sky to separate the day from the night, and let them serve as signs to mark sacred times, and days and years, 15 and let them be lights in the vault of the sky to give light on the earth." And it was so. 16 God made two great lights—the greater light to govern the day and the lesser light to govern the night. He also made the stars. 17 God set them in the vault of the sky to give light on the earth, 18 to govern the day and the night, and to separate light from darkness. And God saw that it was good. 19 And there was evening, and there was morning—the fourth day." (Genesis 1:14-19).

20 "And God said, "Let the water teem with living creatures, and let birds fly above the earth across the vault of the sky." 21 So God created the great creatures of the sea and every living thing with which the water teems and that moves about in it, according to their kinds, and every winged bird according to its kind. And God saw that it was good. 22 God blessed them and said, "Be fruitful and increase in number and fill the water in the seas, and let the birds increase on the earth." 23 And there was evening, and there was morning—the fifth day." (Genesis 1:20-23).

[24] "And God said, "Let the land produce living creatures according to their kinds: the livestock, the creatures that move along the ground, and the wild animals, each according to its kind." And it was so. [25] God made the wild animals according to their kinds, the livestock according to their kinds, and all the creatures that move along the ground according to their kinds. And God saw that it was good." (Genesis 1:24-25).

[26] "Then God said, "Let us make mankind in our image, in our likeness, so that they may rule over the fish in the sea and the birds in the sky, over the livestock and all the wild animals, and over all the creatures that move along the ground." (Genesis 1:26).

[27] "So God created mankind in his own image, in the image of God he created them; male and female he created them. [28] God blessed them and said to them, "Be fruitful and increase in number; fill the earth and subdue it. Rule over the fish in the sea and the birds in the sky and over every living creature that moves on the ground." (Genesis 1:26-28).

[29] "Then God said, "I give you every seed-bearing plant on the face of the whole earth and every tree that has fruit with seed in it. They will be yours for food. [30] And to all the beasts of the earth and all the birds in the sky and all the creatures that move along the ground—everything that has the breath of life in it—I give every green plant for food." And it was so." (Genesis 1:29-30).

[31] God saw all that he had made, and it was very good. And there was evening, and there was morning—the sixth day." (Genesis 1:31).

"Thus the heavens and the earth were completed in all their vast array." (Genesis 2:1).

[2] "By the seventh day God had finished the work he had been doing; so on the seventh day he rested from all his

work. ³ *Then God blessed the seventh day and made it holy, because on it he rested from all the work of creating that he had done." (Genesis 2:2-3).*

In the following section, God provided extra details about the creation of man and woman and their placement in the Garden of Eden which He did not include in Genesis 1:26-30):

⁴ *"This is the account of the heavens and the earth when they were created, when the LORD God made the earth and the heavens." (Genesis 2:4).*

⁵ *Now no shrub had yet appeared on the earth and no plant had yet sprung up, for the LORD God had not sent rain on the earth and there was no one to work the ground,* ⁶ *but streams came up from the earth and watered the whole surface of the ground.* ⁷ *Then the LORD God formed a man from the dust of the ground and breathed into his nostrils the breath of life, and the man became a living being.*

⁸ *Now the LORD God had planted a garden in the east, in Eden; and there he put the man he had formed.* ⁹ *The LORD God made all kinds of trees grow out of the ground—trees that were pleasing to the eye and good for food. In the middle of the garden were the tree of life and the tree of the knowledge of good and evil.*

¹⁰ *A river watering the garden flowed from Eden; from there it was separated into four headwaters.* ¹¹ *The name of the first is the Pishon; it winds through the entire land of Havilah, where there is gold.* ¹² *(The gold of that land is good; aromatic resin and onyx are also there.)* ¹³ *The name of the second river is the Gihon; it winds through the entire land of Cush.* ¹⁴ *The name of the third river is*

the Tigris; it runs along the east side of Ashur. And the fourth river is the Euphrates.

¹⁵ The LORD God took the man and put him in the Garden of Eden to work it and take care of it. ¹⁶ And the LORD God commanded the man, "You are free to eat from any tree in the garden; ¹⁷ but you must not eat from the tree of the knowledge of good and evil, for when you eat from it you will certainly die."

¹⁸ The LORD God said, "It is not good for the man to be alone. I will make a helper suitable for him."

¹⁹ Now the LORD God had formed out of the ground all the wild animals and all the birds in the sky. He brought them to the man to see what he would name them; and whatever the man called each living creature, that was its name. ²⁰ So the man gave names to all the livestock, the birds in the sky and all the wild animals.

But for Adam no suitable helper was found. ²¹ So the LORD God caused the man to fall into a deep sleep; and while he was sleeping, he took one of the man's ribs and then closed up the place with flesh. ²² Then the LORD God made a woman from the rib he had taken out of the man, and he brought her to the man.

²³ The man said,

"This is now bone of my bones
    and flesh of my flesh;
she shall be called 'woman,'
    for she was taken out of man."

²⁴ That is why a man leaves his father and mother and is united to his wife, and they become one flesh.

²⁵ Adam and his wife were both naked, and they felt no shame." (Genesis 2:1-25).

In the Book of JOB:

"Then the LORD spoke to Job out of the storm. He said *(Job 38:1):*

2 **"Who is this that obscures my plans
with words without knowledge?**
3 **Brace yourself like a man;
I will question you,
and you shall answer me.** *(Job 38:2-3).*

4 **"Where were you when I laid the earth's foundation?
Tell me, if you understand.**
5 **Who marked off its dimensions? Surely you know!
Who stretched a measuring line across it?**
6 **On what were its footings set,
or who laid its cornerstone—**
7 **while the morning stars sang together
and all the angels shouted for joy?** *(Job 38:4-7).*

8 **"Who shut up the sea behind doors
when it burst forth from the womb,**
9 **when I made the clouds its garment
and wrapped it in thick darkness,**
10 **when I fixed limits for it
and set its doors and bars in place,**
11 **when I said, 'This far you may come and no farther;
here is where your proud waves halt'?** *(Job 38:8-11).*

12 **"Have you ever given orders to the morning,
or shown the dawn its place,**
13 **that it might take the earth by the edges
and shake the wicked out of it?**
14 **The earth takes shape like clay under a seal;
its features stand out like those of a garment.**

*¹⁵ The wicked are denied their light,
and their upraised arm is broken. (Job 38:12-15).*

*¹⁶ "Have you journeyed to the springs of the sea
or walked in the recesses of the deep?
¹⁷ Have the gates of death been shown to you?
Have you seen the gates of the deepest darkness?
¹⁸ Have you comprehended the vast expanses of the
earth?
Tell me, if you know all this. (Job 38:16-18).*

*¹⁹ "What is the way to the abode of light?
And where does darkness reside?
²⁰ Can you take them to their places?
Do you know the paths to their dwellings?
²¹ Surely you know, for you were already born!
You have lived so many years! (Job 38:19-21).*

*²² "Have you entered the storehouses of the snow
or seen the storehouses of the hail,
²³ which I reserve for times of trouble,
for days of war and battle?
²⁴ What is the way to the place where the lightning is
dispersed,
or the place where the east winds are scattered over
the earth?
²⁵ Who cuts a channel for the torrents of rain,
and a path for the thunderstorm,
²⁶ to water a land where no one lives,
an uninhabited desert,
²⁷ to satisfy a desolate wasteland
and make it sprout with grass?
²⁸ Does the rain have a father?
Who fathers the drops of dew?
²⁹ From whose womb comes the ice?
Who gives birth to the frost from the heavens
³⁰ when the waters become hard as stone,
when the surface of the deep is frozen? (Job 38:22-31).*

*³¹ "Can you bind the chains of the Pleiades?
   Can you loosen Orion's belt?
³² Can you bring forth the constellations in their seasons
   or lead out the Bear with its cubs?
³³ Do you know the laws of the heavens?
   Can you set up God's dominion over the earth? (Job
38:31-33).*

*³⁴ "Can you raise your voice to the clouds
   and cover yourself with a flood of water?
³⁵ Do you send the lightning bolts on their way?
   Do they report to you, 'Here we are'?
³⁶ Who gives the ibis wisdom
   or gives the rooster understanding?
³⁷ Who has the wisdom to count the clouds?
   Who can tip over the water jars of the heavens
³⁸ when the dust becomes hard
   and the clods of earth stick together? (Job 38:34-38).*

*³⁹ "Do you hunt the prey for the lioness
   and satisfy the hunger of the lions
⁴⁰ when they crouch in their dens
   or lie in wait in a thicket?
⁴¹ Who provides food for the raven
   when its young cry out to God
   and wander about for lack of food?" (Job 38:39-41).*

*"Do you know when the mountain goats give birth?
   Do you watch when the doe bears her fawn?
² Do you count the months till they bear?" (Job 39:1-2).
   "Do you know the time they give birth?
³ They crouch down and bring forth their young;
   their labor pains are ended.
⁴ Their young thrive and grow strong in the wilds;
   they leave and do not return." (Job 39:3-4).*

*⁵ "Who let the wild donkey go free?
   Who untied its ropes?
⁶ I gave it the wasteland as its home,
   the salt flats as its habitat.*

⁷ It laughs at the commotion in the town;
*   it does not hear a driver's shout.*
⁸ It ranges the hills for its pasture
*   and searches for any green thing." (Job 39:5-8).*

⁹ "Will the wild ox consent to serve you?
*   Will it stay by your manger at night?*
¹⁰ Can you hold it to the furrow with a harness?
*   Will it till the valleys behind you?*
¹¹ Will you rely on it for its great strength?
*   Will you leave your heavy work to it?*
¹² Can you trust it to haul in your grain
*   and bring it to your threshing floor? (Job 39:9-12).*

¹³ "The wings of the ostrich flap joyfully,
*   though they cannot compare*
*   with the wings and feathers of the stork.*
¹⁴ She lays her eggs on the ground
*   and lets them warm in the sand,*
¹⁵ unmindful that a foot may crush them,
*   that some wild animal may trample them.*
¹⁶ She treats her young harshly, as if they were not hers;
*   she cares not that her labor was in vain,*
¹⁷ for God did not endow her with wisdom
*   or give her a share of good sense.*
¹⁸ Yet when she spreads her feathers to run,
*   she laughs at horse and rider. (Job 39:13-18).*

¹⁹ "Do you give the horse its strength
*   or clothe its neck with a flowing mane?*
²⁰ Do you make it leap like a locust,
*   striking terror with its proud snorting?*
²¹ It paws fiercely, rejoicing in its strength,
*   and charges into the fray.*
²² It laughs at fear, afraid of nothing;
*   it does not shy away from the sword.*
²³ The quiver rattles against its side,
*   along with the flashing spear and lance. (Job 39:19-23).*
²⁴ In frenzied excitement it eats up the ground;
*   it cannot stand still when the trumpet sounds.*

[25] **At the blast of the trumpet it snorts, 'Aha!'**
   It catches the scent of battle from afar,
   the shout of commanders and the battle cry. *(Job 39:24-25).*

[26] **"Does the hawk take flight by your wisdom**
   and spread its wings toward the south?
[27] **Does the eagle soar at your command**
   and build its nest on high?
[28] **It dwells on a cliff and stays there at night;**
   a rocky crag is its stronghold.
[29] **From there it looks for food;**
   its eyes detect it from afar.
[30] **Its young ones feast on blood,**
   and where the slain are, there it is." *(Job 39:26-30).*

The LORD said to Job *(Job 40:1):*

[2] **"Will the one who contends with the Almighty correct him?**
   Let him who accuses God answer him!" *(Job 40:2)*

[3] **Then Job answered the LORD***(Job 40:3):*

[4] **"I am unworthy—how can I reply to you?**
   I put my hand over my mouth.
[5] **I spoke once, but I have no answer—**
   twice, but I will say no more." *(Job 40:4-5).*

[6] **Then the LORD spoke to Job out of the storm***(Job 40:6):*

[7] **"Brace yourself like a man;**
   I will question you,
   and you shall answer me. *(Job 40:7).*

[8] **"Would you discredit my justice?**
   Would you condemn me to justify yourself?
[9] **Do you have an arm like God's,**
   and can your voice thunder like his?
[10] **Then adorn yourself with glory and splendor,**

and clothe yourself in honor and majesty.
[11] Unleash the fury of your wrath,
look at all who are proud and bring them low,
[12] look at all who are proud and humble them,
crush the wicked where they stand.
[13] Bury them all in the dust together;
shroud their faces in the grave. (Job 40:8-13).
[14] Then I myself will admit to you
that your own right hand can save you. (Job 40:14)

[15] "Look at Behemoth,
which I made along with you
and which feeds on grass like an ox.
[16] What strength it has in its loins,
what power in the muscles of its belly!
[17] Its tail sways like a cedar;
the sinews of its thighs are close-knit.
[18] Its bones are tubes of bronze,
its limbs like rods of iron.
[19] It ranks first among the works of God,
yet its Maker can approach it with his sword.
[20] The hills bring it their produce,
and all the wild animals play nearby.
[21] Under the lotus plants it lies,
hidden among the reeds in the marsh.
[22] The lotuses conceal it in their shadow;
the poplars by the stream surround it.
[23] A raging river does not alarm it;
it is secure, though the Jordan should surge against its
mouth.
[24] Can anyone capture it by the eyes,
or trap it and pierce its nose?" (Job 40:15-24).

[1] "Can you pull in Leviathan with a fishhook
or tie down its tongue with a rope? (Job 41:1).
[2] Can you put a cord through its nose
or pierce its jaw with a hook?
[3] Will it keep begging you for mercy?
Will it speak to you with gentle words?
[4] Will it make an agreement with you

for you to take it as your slave for life?
5 Can you make a pet of it like a bird
    or put it on a leash for the young women in your house?
6 Will traders barter for it?
    Will they divide it up among the merchants?
7 Can you fill its hide with harpoons
    or its head with fishing spears?
8 If you lay a hand on it,
    you will remember the struggle and never do it again!
9 Any hope of subduing it is false;
    the mere sight of it is overpowering.
10 No one is fierce enough to rouse it.
    Who then is able to stand against me?
11 Who has a claim against me that I must pay?
    Everything under heaven belongs to me. (Job 41:2-11).

12 "I will not fail to speak of Leviathan's limbs,
    its strength and its graceful form.
13 Who can strip off its outer coat?
    Who can penetrate its double coat of armor[b]?
14 Who dares open the doors of its mouth,
    ringed about with fearsome teeth?
15 Its back has[c] rows of shields
    tightly sealed together;
16 each is so close to the next
    that no air can pass between.
17 They are joined fast to one another;
    they cling together and cannot be parted.
18 Its snorting throws out flashes of light;
    its eyes are like the rays of dawn.
19 Flames stream from its mouth;
    sparks of fire shoot out.
20 Smoke pours from its nostrils
    as from a boiling pot over burning reeds.
21 Its breath sets coals ablaze,
    and flames dart from its mouth.
22 Strength resides in its neck;
    dismay goes before it.
23 The folds of its flesh are tightly joined;
    they are firm and immovable.

[24] Its chest is hard as rock,
   hard as a lower millstone.
[25] When it rises up, the mighty are terrified;
   they retreat before its thrashing.
[26] The sword that reaches it has no effect,
   nor does the spear or the dart or the javelin.
[27] Iron it treats like straw
   and bronze like rotten wood.
[28] Arrows do not make it flee;
   slingstones are like chaff to it.
[29] A club seems to it but a piece of straw;
   it laughs at the rattling of the lance.
[30] Its undersides are jagged potsherds,
   leaving a trail in the mud like a threshing sledge.
[31] It makes the depths churn like a boiling caldron
   and stirs up the sea like a pot of ointment.
[32] It leaves a glistening wake behind it;
   one would think the deep had white hair.
[33] Nothing on earth is its equal—
   a creature without fear.
[34] It looks down on all that are haughty;
   it is king over all that are proud." (Job 41:12-34).

"Then Job replied to the LORD (Job 42:1):

[2] "I know that you can do all things;
   no purpose of yours can be thwarted.
[3] You asked, 'Who is this that obscures my plans without
knowledge?'
   Surely I spoke of things I did not understand,
   things too wonderful for me to know. (Job 42:2-3).

[4] "You said, 'Listen now, and I will speak;
   I will question you,
   and you shall answer me.'
[5] My ears had heard of you
   but now my eyes have seen you.
[6] Therefore I despise myself
   and repent in dust and ashes." (Job 42:4-6).

In the Book of ISAIAH:

""*This is what the L*ORD *says—*
  your Redeemer, who formed you in the womb:

   *I am the L*ORD,
   the Maker of all things,
   who stretches out the heavens,
   who spreads out the earth by myself,
25 who foils the signs of false prophets
   and makes fools of diviners,
who overthrows the learning of the wise
   and turns it into nonsense,
26 who carries out the words of his servants
   and fulfills the predictions of his messengers,

who says of Jerusalem, 'It shall be inhabited,'
   of the towns of Judah, 'They shall be rebuilt,'
   and of their ruins, 'I will restore them,'
27 who says to the watery deep, 'Be dry,
   and I will dry up your streams,'" (Isaiah 44:24-27).

"I am the LORD, and there is no other.
7 I form the light and create darkness,
  I bring prosperity and create disaster;
  I, the LORD, do all these things." *(Isaiah 45:6-7)*

It is I who made the earth
   and created mankind on it.
My own hands stretched out the heavens;
   I marshaled their starry hosts. ´ *(Isaiah 45:12-13).*

"For this is what the LORD says—
he who created the heavens,
   he is God;

he who fashioned and made the earth,
    he founded it;
he did not create it to be empty,
    but formed it to be inhabited—
he says:
"I am the LORD,
    and there is no other.
[19] I have not spoken in secret,
    from somewhere in a land of darkness;
I have not said to Jacob's descendants,
    'Seek me in vain.'
I, the LORD, speak the truth;
    I declare what is right.

[20] "Gather together and come;
    assemble, you fugitives from the nations.
Ignorant are those who carry about idols of wood,
    who pray to gods that cannot save.
[21] Declare what is to be, present it—
    let them take counsel together.
Who foretold this long ago,
    who declared it from the distant past?
Was it not I, the LORD?
    And there is no God apart from me,
a righteous God and a Savior;
    there is none but me.

[22] "Turn to me and be saved,
    all you ends of the earth;
    for I am God, and there is no other.
[23] By myself I have sworn,
    my mouth has uttered in all integrity
    a word that will not be revoked:
Before me every knee will bow;
    by me every tongue will swear.
[24] They will say of me, 'In the LORD alone
    are deliverance and strength.'"
All who have raged against him
    will come to him and be put to shame.
[25] But all the descendants of Israel

will find deliverance in the LORD
and will make their boast in him." *(Isaiah 45:18-25).*

""Remember this, keep it in mind,
  take it to heart, you rebels.
[9] Remember the former things, those of long ago;
  I am God, and there is no other;
  I am God, and there is none like me.
[10] I make known the end from the beginning,
  from ancient times, what is still to come.
I say, 'My purpose will stand,
  and I will do all that I please.'
[11] From the east I summon a bird of prey;
  from a far-off land, a man to fulfill my purpose.
What I have said, that I will bring about;
  what I have planned, that I will do.
[12] Listen to me, you stubborn-hearted,
  you who are now far from my righteousness.
[13] I am bringing my righteousness near,
  it is not far away;
  and my salvation will not be delayed.
I will grant salvation to Zion,
  my splendor to Israel." (Isaiah 46:8-13).

"You said, 'I am forever—
  the eternal queen!'
But you did not consider these things
  or reflect on what might happen.

[8] "Now then, listen, you lover of pleasure,
  lounging in your security
and saying to yourself,
  'I am, and there is none besides me.
I will never be a widow
  or suffer the loss of children.'
[9] Both of these will overtake you
  in a moment, on a single day:
  loss of children and widowhood.
They will come upon you in full measure,

in spite of your many sorceries
and all your potent spells.
[10] You have trusted in your wickedness
and have said, 'No one sees me.'
Your wisdom and knowledge mislead you
when you say to yourself,
'I am, and there is none besides me.'
[11] Disaster will come upon you,
and you will not know how to conjure it away.
A calamity will fall upon you
that you cannot ward off with a ransom;
a catastrophe you cannot foresee
will suddenly come upon you.

[12] "Keep on, then, with your magic spells
and with your many sorceries,
which you have labored at since childhood.
Perhaps you will succeed,
perhaps you will cause terror.
[13] All the counsel you have received has only worn you out!
Let your astrologers come forward,
those stargazers who make predictions month by month,
let them save you from what is coming upon you.
[14] Surely they are like stubble;
the fire will burn them up.
They cannot even save themselves
from the power of the flame.
These are not coals for warmth;
this is not a fire to sit by.
[15] That is all they are to you—
these you have dealt with
and labored with since childhood.
All of them go on in their error;
there is not one that can save you." *(Isaiah 47:7-15).*

**"I foretold the former things long ago,
my mouth announced them and I made them known;
then suddenly I acted, and they came to pass.
[4] For I knew how stubborn you were;
your neck muscles were iron,**

your forehead was bronze.
5 Therefore I told you these things long ago;
   before they happened I announced them to you
so that you could not say,
   'My images brought them about;
   my wooden image and metal god ordained them.'
6 You have heard these things; look at them all.
   Will you not admit them?

"From now on I will tell you of new things,
   of hidden things unknown to you.
7 They are created now, and not long ago;
   you have not heard of them before today.
So you cannot say,
   'Yes, I knew of them.'
8 You have neither heard nor understood;
   from of old your ears have not been open.
Well do I know how treacherous you are;
   you were called a rebel from birth.
9 For my own name's sake I delay my wrath;
   for the sake of my praise I hold it back from you,
   so as not to destroy you completely.
10 See, I have refined you, though not as silver;
   I have tested you in the furnace of affliction.
11 For my own sake, for my own sake, I do this.
   How can I let myself be defamed?
   I will not yield my glory to another.

12 "Listen to me, Jacob,
   Israel, whom I have called:
I am he;
   I am the first and I am the last.
13 My own hand laid the foundations of the earth,
   and my right hand spread out the heavens;
when I summon them,
   they all stand up together.

14 "Come together, all of you, and listen:
   Which of the idols has foretold these things?
The LORD's chosen ally
   will carry out his purpose against Babylon;
   his arm will be against the Babylonians.
15 I, even I, have spoken;

yes, I have called him.
I will bring him,
  and he will succeed in his mission.

[16] "Come near me and listen to this:

"From the first announcement I have not spoken in secret;
  at the time it happens, I am there."

And now the Sovereign LORD has sent me,
  endowed with his Spirit.

[17] This is what the LORD says—
  your Redeemer, the Holy One of Israel:
"I am the LORD your God,
  who teaches you what is best for you,
  who directs you in the way you should go.
[18] If only you had paid attention to my commands,
  your peace would have been like a river,
  your well-being like the waves of the sea.
[19] Your descendants would have been like the sand,
  your children like its numberless grains;
their name would never be blotted out
  nor destroyed from before me."

[20] Leave Babylon,
  flee from the Babylonians!
Announce this with shouts of joy
  and proclaim it.
Send it out to the ends of the earth;
  say, "The LORD has redeemed his servant Jacob."
[21] They did not thirst when he led them through the deserts;
  he made water flow for them from the rock;
he split the rock
  and water gushed out.

[22] "There is no peace," says the LORD, "for the wicked."" *(Isaiah 48:3-22).*

"Can plunder be taken from warriors,
or captives be rescued from the fierce

[25] *But this is what the L*ORD *says:*

"Yes, captives will be taken from warriors,
and plunder retrieved from the fierce;
I will contend with those who contend with you,
and your children I will save.
[26] *I will make your oppressors eat their own flesh;*
they will be drunk on their own blood, as with wine.
Then all mankind will know
*that I, the L*ORD, *am your Savior,*
your Redeemer, the Mighty One of Jacob."" *(Isaiah 49:24-26).*

"When I came, why was there no one?
    When I called, why was there no one to answer?
Was my arm too short to deliver you?
    Do I lack the strength to rescue you?
By a mere rebuke I dry up the sea,
    I turn rivers into a desert;
their fish rot for lack of water
    and die of thirst.
[3] I clothe the heavens with darkness
    and make sackcloth its covering."" *(Isaiah 50:2-3).*

"Listen to me, you who pursue righteousness
*and who seek the L*ORD*:*
Look to the rock from which you were cut
and to the quarry from which you were hewn." (Isaiah 51:1).

""Listen to me, my people;
    hear me, my nation:
Instruction will go out from me;
    my justice will become a light to the nations.
[5] My righteousness draws near speedily,
    my salvation is on the way,

and my arm will bring justice to the nations.
The islands will look to me
 and wait in hope for my arm.
⁶ Lift up your eyes to the heavens,
 look at the earth beneath;
the heavens will vanish like smoke,
 the earth will wear out like a garment
 and its inhabitants die like flies.
But my salvation will last forever,
 my righteousness will never fail." *(Isaiah 51:4-6).*

"Awake, awake, arm of the LORD,
 clothe yourself with strength!
Awake, as in days gone by,
 as in generations of old.
Was it not you who cut Rahab to pieces,
 who pierced that monster through?
¹⁰ *Was it not you who dried up the sea,*
 the waters of the great deep,
who made a road in the depths of the sea
 so that the redeemed might cross over?" (Isaiah 51:9-10).

"For I am the LORD your God,
 who stirs up the sea so that its waves roar—
 the LORD Almighty is his name." *(Isaiah 51:15).*

I have put my words in your mouth
 and covered you with the shadow of my hand—
I who set the heavens in place,
 who laid the foundations of the earth,
 and who say to Zion, 'You are my people.'"" (Isaiah 51:16).

"See, my servant will act wisely;
 he will be raised and lifted up and highly exalted.
¹⁴ *Just as there were many who were appalled at him—*
 his appearance was so disfigured beyond that of any human

being
    and his form marred beyond human likeness—
[15] **so he will sprinkle many nations,**
    and kings will shut their mouths because of him.
For what they were not told, they will see,
    and what they have not heard, they will understand." *(Isaiah 52:13-15).*

"Who has believed our message
    and to whom has the arm of the LORD been revealed?
[2] He grew up before him like a tender shoot,
    and like a root out of dry ground.
He had no beauty or majesty to attract us to him,
    nothing in his appearance that we should desire him.
[3] He was despised and rejected by mankind,
    a man of suffering, and familiar with pain.
Like one from whom people hide their faces
    he was despised, and we held him in low esteem."
(Isaiah 53:1-3).

[4] "Surely he took up our pain
    and bore our suffering,
yet we considered him punished by God,
    stricken by him, and afflicted.
[5] But he was pierced for our transgressions,
    he was crushed for our iniquities;
the punishment that brought us peace was on him,
    and by his wounds we are healed.
[6] We all, like sheep, have gone astray,
    each of us has turned to our own way;
and the LORD has laid on him
    the iniquity of us all." *(Isaiah 53:4-6).*

[7] "He was oppressed and afflicted,
    yet he did not open his mouth;
he was led like a lamb to the slaughter,
    and as a sheep before its shearers is silent,

so he did not open his mouth.
[8] By oppression and judgment he was taken away.
   Yet who of his generation protested?
For he was cut off from the land of the living;
   for the transgression of my people he was punished.
[9] He was assigned a grave with the wicked,
   and with the rich in his death,
though he had done no violence,
   nor was any deceit in his mouth." *(Isaiah 53:7-9).*

[10]"Yet it was the LORD's will to crush him and cause him to suffer,
   and though the LORD makes his life an offering for sin,
he will see his offspring and prolong his days,
   and the will of the LORD will prosper in his hand.
[11] After he has suffered,
   he will see the light of life and be satisfied;
by his knowledge my righteous servant will justify many,
   and he will bear their iniquities.
[12] Therefore I will give him a portion among the great,
   and he will divide the spoils with the strong,
because he poured out his life unto death,
   and was numbered with the transgressors.
For he bore the sin of many,
   and made intercession for the transgressors." *(Isaiah 53:10-12).*

'"See, it is I who created the blacksmith
   who fans the coals into flame
   and forges a weapon fit for its work.
And it is I who have created the destroyer to wreak havoc;
[17]   *no weapon forged against you will prevail,*
   and you will refute every tongue that accuses you.
This is the heritage of the servants of the LORD,
   and this is their vindication from me,"
declares the LORD.'" (Isaiah 54:16-17).

"Seek the LORD while he may be found;
   call on him while he is near.

⁷ Let the wicked forsake their ways
    and the unrighteous their thoughts.
Let them turn to the LORD, and he will have mercy on them,
    and to our God, for he will freely pardon." *(Isaiah 55:6-7).*

⁸ "For my thoughts are not your thoughts,
    neither are your ways my ways,"
declares the LORD.
⁹ "As the heavens are higher than the earth,
    so are my ways higher than your ways
    and my thoughts than your thoughts.
¹⁰ As the rain and the snow
    come down from heaven,
and do not return to it
    without watering the earth
and making it bud and flourish,
    so that it yields seed for the sower and bread for the eater,
¹¹ so is my word that goes out from my mouth:
    It will not return to me empty,
but will accomplish what I desire
    and achieve the purpose for which I sent it." *(Isaiah 55:8-11).*

"For this is what the high and exalted One says—
    he who lives forever, whose name is holy:
"I live in a high and holy place,
    but also with the one who is contrite and lowly in spirit,
to revive the spirit of the lowly
    and to revive the heart of the contrite.
¹⁶ *I will not accuse them forever,*
    nor will I always be angry,
for then they would faint away because of me—
    the very people I have created." (Isaiah 57:15-16).

Who is this coming from Edom,
    from Bozrah, with his garments stained crimson?
Who is this, robed in splendor,
    striding forward in the greatness of his strength? "It is I,
proclaiming victory,
    mighty to save." ² Why are your garments red,
    like those of one treading the winepress?" *(Isaiah 63:1-2).*

³ "I have trodden the winepress alone;
    from the nations no one was with me.
I trampled them in my anger
    and trod them down in my wrath;
their blood spattered my garments,
    and I stained all my clothing.
⁴ It was for me the day of vengeance;
    the year for me to redeem had come.
⁵ I looked, but there was no one to help,
    I was appalled that no one gave support;
so my own arm achieved salvation for me,
    and my own wrath sustained me.
⁶ I trampled the nations in my anger;
    in my wrath I made them drunk
    and poured their blood on the ground." *(Isaiah 63:3-6).*

*"See, I will create
  new heavens and a new earth.
The former things will not be remembered,
  nor will they come to mind."* (Isaiah 65:17).

""Heaven is my throne,
    and the earth is my footstool.
Where is the house you will build for me?
    Where will my resting place be?
² Has not my hand made all these things,
    and so they came into being?"
declares the LORD. "These are the ones I look on with favor:
    those who are humble and contrite in spirit,
    and who tremble at my word.
³ But whoever sacrifices a bull
    is like one who kills a person,
and whoever offers a lamb
    is like one who breaks a dog's neck;
whoever makes a grain offering
    is like one who presents pig's blood,
and whoever burns memorial incense

is like one who worships an idol.
They have chosen their own ways,
   and they delight in their abominations;
4 so I also will choose harsh treatment for them
   and will bring on them what they dread.
For when I called, no one answered,
   when I spoke, no one listened.
They did evil in my sight
   and chose what displeases me." *(Isaiah 66:1-4).*

5 Hear the word of the LORD,
   you who tremble at his word:
"Your own people who hate you,
   and exclude you because of my name, have said,
'Let the LORD be glorified,
   that we may see your joy!'
   Yet they will be put to shame.
6 Hear that uproar from the city,
   hear that noise from the temple!
It is the sound of the LORD
   repaying his enemies all they deserve." *(Isaiah 66:5-6).*

"As the new heavens and the new earth that I make will endure before me," declares the LORD, "so will your name and descendants endure. 23 From one New Moon to another and from one Sabbath to another, all mankind will come and bow down before me," says the LORD. 24 "And they will go out and look on the dead bodies of those who rebelled against me; the worms that eat them will not die, the fire that burns them will not be quenched, and they will be loathsome to all mankind." *(Isaiah 66:22-24).*

Chapter 3

Let There Be Light, And There Was Light!

The Bible starts: *"In the beginning God created the heavens and the earth. ² Now the earth was formless and empty, darkness was over the surface of the deep, and the Spirit of God was hovering over the waters. ³ And God said, "Let there be light," and there was light. ⁴ God saw that the light was good, and he separated the light from the darkness. ⁵ God called the light "day," and the darkness he called "night." And there was evening, and there was morning—the first day. (Genesis 1:1-5).*

⁶ "And God said, Let there be a firmament in the midst of the waters, and let it divide the waters from the waters. ⁷ And God made the firmament, and divided the waters which were under the firmament from the waters which were above the firmament: and it was so. ⁸ And God called the firmament Heaven. And the evening and the morning were the second day." (Genesis 1:6-8).

⁹ "And God said, Let the waters under the heaven be gathered together unto one place, and let the dry land appear: and it was so. ¹⁰ And God called the dry land Earth; and the gathering together of the waters called he Seas: and God saw that it was good. ¹¹ And God said, Let the earth bring forth grass, the herb yielding seed, and the fruit tree yielding fruit after his kind, whose seed is in itself, upon the earth: and it was so. ¹² And the earth brought forth grass, and herb yielding seed after his kind, and the tree yielding fruit, whose seed was in itself, after his kind: and God saw that it was good. [13] And the evening and the morning were the third day." (Genesis 1:9-13).

According to the passage above, the earth is the center of the universe and the beginning of it all! God first created the earth—with malleable land forming the core and a deluge of water covering over the entire land; and the earth was 'formless' and 'empty'. At this point neither time nor space was in existence—just the earth under water. *(Genesis 1:1-2).*

At this point— Genesis 1:1-2—there were God the Father, God the Son and God the Holy Spirit *(Genesis 1:2)* and *(John 1:1-2)*. There were also the angels of God. *(Job 38:4-7)*. And the only thing that was created by God up to this point was the earth that was still under water. But there were no time, no space, no sun, no moon, and no stars. And there was none of the other heavenly bodies we know or see today.

And then at Genesis 1:3, God created time by ushering in the light: *[3] "And God said, "Let there be light," and there was light. [4] God saw that the light was good, and he separated the light from the darkness. [5] God called the light "day," and the darkness he called "night." And there was evening, and there was morning—the first day. (Genesis 1:3-5).* This is the birth of time and it started ticking away. God gave birth to time through His Son Jesus Christ who put the light upon the young earth to provide not just visualization but also life and enlightenment onto the earth.

Jesus started time in Genesis 1:3, when at God's command, He became light on Day 1 of the creation and lit up the face of the earth. And Jesus Christ will end time in

Revelation 22:5, when there is no more night and no need for the light of a lamp or the light of the sun, and He becomes the everlasting light for the saved. Jesus Christ is indeed the beginning and the end!

Then on the second day—one day after time debuted—God created space: *⁶ "And God said, Let there be a firmament in the midst of the waters, and let it divide the waters from the waters. ⁷ And God made the firmament, and divided the waters which were under the firmament from the waters which were above the firmament: and it was so. ⁸ And God called the firmament Heaven. And the evening and the morning were the second day." (Genesis 1:6-8).*

This is the birth of space—the entirety of it as we know it today. Nothing was added to it or taken away from it from that moment till now. And nothing will be added to it or taken away from it until God decides to end it all. God created space once and it was created perfectly; and perfectly bound by water on the larger outer perimeter, with the earth and its waters on the inner perimeter. *And God made the firmament, and divided the waters which were under the firmament from the waters which were above the firmament: and it was so. ⁸ And God called the firmament Heaven (Genesis 1:7-8).*

Make no mistake about it; there are oceans of water beyond space. The water above the firmament stays above the firmament and never reentered into our universe. God said that in this passage and if it were not so, He would not have said it. If anyone were to see that ocean of water above the firmament, that person would have to travel out of this universe to see it And the heaven in which God resides in, is outside of our universe as well.

The current effort by scientists across the world to find water somewhere else in the universe to prove that God does not exist is a wasteful enterprise. They got the wrong interpretation of the Genesis account of creation. As a matter of fact, we all got it wrong. Even us, who believe in God, thought that the deep space was all there is from God's creation because of the sheer size of it.

And the naysayers did not make it easy by constantly teasing Christian's about the little t they knew about the earth and the universe prior to advent of science and astronomy. And since they seem to have the superior knowledge Christians became very cautious not to speak in embarrassment And the great advanced products and services produced through science and technology made the scientists appear to have it all figured out. But in reality, what science does is employ assumptions and extrapolations; which at their best, yield approximate results.

That is why things that are fabricated through science and technology fail from time to time. Human perfection shoots for 'best possible yield'. And because no human being comes anywhere close to perfection, the 'best possible yield' becomes wildly acceptable. We have 365¼ days to make a year. And we all know that God never created ¼ of a day. All seven days of creation in Genesis are full days and no fraction. So we approximate even in the most central things in our lives.

But the things built and positioned by God never produce approximate results, unless they have been tainted through our sinfulness. They work all of the time and yield 100% accuracy all the time. God is perfection and everything He creates is perfect. And God is not temperamental but sticks to His plan despite human insults and meddling, because He is supremely confident that His plan will hold.

The earth was round at Genesis 1:1-3, and is still round. The earth in its entirety was covered with a huge deluge of water. To divide water from water all around the earth requires that a sphere be introduced inside the water to sit between the spherical earth and its water, and the rest of the water above the new sphere. The purpose of the sphere in-between waters was to create space.

God introduced a spherical void into the 'waters' and separated the water immediately surrounding the earth from the rest of the water now sitting atop the spherical void. This void is fitted around the earth and its water—as one would make a garment to completely cover a spherical object—thereby encapsulating the earth its water. And the rest of the water sits atop the spherical void: *And God made the firmament, and divided the waters which were under the firmament from the waters which were above the firmament: and it was so. [8] And God called the firmament Heaven (Genesis 1:7-8).*

God introduced this new spherical void just like a preform—as in today's blow-molding operations. He then expanded the void, pushing the water atop the void farther and farther out until the void reached the size God desired: **"It is I who made the earth and created mankind on it. My own hands stretched out the heavens; I marshaled their starry hosts."** *(Isaiah 45:12).*

And because the void was completely submersed inside water it becomes like a bubble trapped in water—a spherical void which encapsulated the earth and its waters. As God expanded the void, He created a vacuum inside the void, forming rigid walls of water throughout the entire dimensions of the void to maintain the vacuum within the expanded void.

In the natural, this kind of expansion is impossible. But I will illustrate with an elastic pouch with closed ends—say deflated balloon with its end tied and completely submersed in water. Stretched the elastic pouch while it is still fully submersed causes the elastic pouch to elongate and create more surface area within the pouch due to increased. This increase in the surface area (potential space) within the pouch would not necessarily translate into more water being displaced.

And by introducing just enough pressure inside the stretched out elastic pouch to prevent the extended pouch from going back to its relaxed state, the inside surface area automatically transforms into actual space and stays extended. Stretching a balloon before air is blown into it reduces the force at which the incoming air impacts the walls of the balloon thereby reducing the chance of the balloon rupturing. The air going into the balloon also will experience less resistance by the walls of the balloon thereby allowing the air to move faster and farther within the balloon.

And when the goal is to first explode concentrated energy inside the elastic pouch and occupy the inside of the elastic pouch with flaming balls of fire, stretching the elastic pouch to a capacity that is beyond your estimated energy dispersion becomes imperative or your explosion would completely destroy the elastic pouch. But this is how we do things in the natural.

But God is supernatural and has perfect knowledge of all things, and creates all things. So He could make for Himself anything He desires and impart on that thing whatever properties He chooses to impart on it. He carried out the expansion of the firmament inside water and could maintain the resulting void under vacuum if He chose to, since the waters would have created a perfect seal on all points around the spherical void to keep everything else out of the void. *(Genesis 1:7)*. With His space under vacuum, it was time for the next step in His creation project.

The purpose of my little demonstration above is to help the scientist in all of us to see the information that is there but does not immediately jump out of the page. That way, we'll have more confident in God's own presentation of His awesome design and execution. It is stupid to second guess what God might or might not have done. God gave me discernment and the various facts that were strewn all over the Bible about creation began to come together as pieces of puzzle as I was once again going through this page of God's great Book.

My task here is to shed a little more light on the accuracy of what God recorded for us in this wonderful Book of Genesis. There are so many people in the world who are better trained and more qualified than I to give more insights into this record in Genesis. And it is my express hope that those people will come along and help the world understand the care and the expertise God put into designing and building the earth and the entire universe.

God did not make mankind for the earth; God made the earth and everything in the earth for mankind; because of His love for all humanity. Why? Because He put His Spirit in us and made us in His own image so that we will be His children! And because we did not choose to be made; He chose to make us, love us and care for us.

The universe was created on Day four to accommodate, and put in constant display, the awesome power of the Almighty God. ***"And God said, Let there be lights in the firmament of the heaven to divide the day from the night; and let them be for signs ...,"*** *(Genesis 1:14);* and not so mankind would start chasing the shadows, bent on discrediting God. If Jesus Christ had directly remained the light for the earth as he did from Day 1 through Day 3, humanity would not be able to survive on the earth; because His intensity as light, fire and heat would have incinerated all mankind.

So Jesus Christ separated part of the light that was in Him into trillions of quasi and stars and spread them across space. Out of those trillions of stars that now burn with His fire, His light and His vitality; He set the smallest of them in our solar system—the sun—to power life on the earth and support all the other planets in the solar system that were put there to benefit us in ways we will never fully understand.

Pay particular attention to the underlined sections of the following passages: [6] *"**And God said, Let there be a firmament in the midst of the waters**, and let it divide the waters from the waters.* [7] *And God made the firmament, and divided the waters which were under the firmament from the waters which were above the firmament: and it was so.* [8] *And God called the firmament Heaven. And the evening and the morning were the second day."* (Genesis 1:6-8).

*"**And God said, Let there be lights in the firmament of the heaven** to divide the day from the night; **and let them be for signs**, and for seasons, and for days, and years:* [15] *And let them be for lights in the firmament of the heaven to give light upon the earth: and it was so.* [16] *And God made two great lights; the greater light to rule the day, and the lesser light to rule the night: he made the stars also.* [17] *And God set them in the firmament of the heaven to give light upon the earth,* [18] *And to rule over the day and over the night, and to divide the light from the darkness: and God saw that it was good.* [19] *And the evening and the morning were the fourth day".* (Genesis 1:14-19).

Here is what the underlined sections of the preceding passages look like condensed out of the passages: *"And God said, Let there be a firmament in the midst of the waters ... And God called the firmament Heaven."* (Genesis 1:6-8). *"And God said, Let there be lights in the firmament of the heaven ... and let them be for signs ..."* (Genesis 1:14-19). And this clearly shows that the universe was created on Day 4 to accommodate and put in constant display the awesome power of the Almighty God.

So there you have it. The Trinity and all the heavenly hosts were around before the earth was created. And to make the earth, God started with water and a 'blob' of earth that he had completely submersed under water. Then He commanded for light and His Son Jesus Christ who had life and light in Him became the light *(John 1:3-5)*, kicking off the dawn of time.

The Next day—Day 2— God called for space and stretched it out. And He called it heaven. The Father commands and the Son promptly executes, *(John 1:3)*, even though on this day the Bible says that **"God made the firmament, and divided the waters which were under the firmament from the waters which were above the firmament: and it was so."** *(Genesis 1:7)*. The Bible also calls the Son, God.

And on Day 3, God commanded for land to appear and be separated from the water to create land and sea. Land developed and was separated from the sea. This was achieved again through His Son Jesus Christ *(John 1:3)*; and possibly through the most intensive and extensive volcanic eruptions never ever again seen on the face of the earth, coupled with clapping tsunamis that roared through earth's waters and echoed throughout space.

On Day 4, God for the second time commanded for lights, but this time to be set in the firmament of heaven. This stage in God's creation is what scientists and astronomers today describes as the Big Band happened that formed the universe. This Big Bang—and trust me there is no other Big Bang that gave birth to the universe—was not started from some 'primordial atom'.

This Big Bang is the Spirit called Jesus Christ, God the Son. And the originator of this Big Bang is well known because He guarantees us that He did it and that He does everything; and He is God! He is the only force in the entire universe. Every other force in the universe is a satellite off of Him, and there is no exception to this rule.

And while they had gotten it right in the sense that the initiation of the dispersion of flaming balls of fire shuttling at incredible speeds through space could make nothing other than the most deafening sound; they got it wrong by insinuating that it happened on its own out of chance. Invocation of chance has become a pretense for wealth acquisition and fame.

And as long as huge financial rewards and fame continues to go to the people who cook up this kind of nonsense, there is no discouragement for them to stop the madness. More than anything else, it has become a money game that positions powerful world governments as humanity's last hope for survival; and continues to make the doomsday prophets rich and famous.

But we must all remember that nothing escapes God in His universe. If He did not authorize it, it would not have happened. He is the Almighty God, and apart from Him, there is no God *(Isaiah 45:21)*. And we see in Genesis 1:6-19 that He authorized this event and was there to oversee it and bring it to astounding completion and majesty. It is His masterpiece set to induce wonders in the minds of all mankind, and it does.

So, at the Father's command, Jesus Christ—the light who appeared on Day 1—cataclysmically dispersed as balls of fire throughout the space that God had 'stretched' out on Day 2, creating galaxies and orbits, setting bodies in perpetual motions and instituting orders throughout space. That is why the Bible says:

"***There is one body and one Spirit, just as you were called to one hope when you were called; [5] one Lord, one faith, one baptism; [6] one God and Father of all, who is over all*** *and through all and in all. ⁷ But to each one of us grace has been given as Christ apportioned it. ⁸ This is why it⁽ᵃ⁾ says: "When he ascended on high, he took many captives and gave gifts to his people."⁽ᵇ⁾ ⁹ (What does "he ascended" mean except that he also descended to the lower, earthly regions⁽ᶜ⁾? ¹⁰ <u>He who descended is the very one who ascended higher than all the heavens, in order to fill the whole universe.</u>)." (Ephesians 4:4-10).*

Day 4 completes the birth of the universe that was started by God on Day 2 when He created space in anticipation of the dispersed energies of Day 4. The stars, the sun, the moon and all the other celestial bodies in space all came into existence on Day 4 and started operating according to the order Jesus Christ set around each cluster. God's showcase was put into a permanent display by His Son Jesus Christ *(John 1:3)*, and the Bible says: ***"And God saw that it was good."*** *(Genesis 1:18).*

The earth was 'formless', because the land mass was molten as in volcanic lava that was still churning. And God covered this huge volcanic mass with water to cool the crust. That is why God said in Job:"-¹⁴ ***<u>The earth takes shape like clay under a seal</u>; its features stand out like those of a garment."*** *(Job 38:14).*

And in Isaiah He said: ***"Listen to me, Jacob, Israel, whom I have called: I am he; I am the first and I am the last. <u>My own hand laid the foundations of the earth</u>, and my right hand spread out the heavens; when I summon them, they all stand up together."*** *(Isaiah 48:12-13).*

<u>"Woe to those who quarrel with their Maker, those who are nothing but potsherds among the potsherds on the ground</u>. Does the clay say to the potter, 'What are you making?' Does your work say, 'The potter has no hands'? ¹⁰ Woe to the one who says to a father, 'What have you begotten?' or to a mother, 'What have you brought to

birth?'" *(Isaiah 45:9-10).*

[11] **"This is what the** L<small>ORD</small> **says—the Holy One of Israel, and its Maker:**
Concerning things to come, do you question me about my children, or give me orders about the work of my hands?
[12] **It is I who made the earth and created mankind on it.**
My own hands stretched out the heavens; I marshaled their starry hosts." *(Isaiah 45:11-12).*

The earth, being 'formless' and its entire surface being covered with water, required containment. Water being a fluid had to be contained within something. Therefore **the Spirit of God was hovering over the waters** *(Genesis 1:2)*—to contain it and to impart God's blessing on water as the foundation of life on the earth. Today in science and astronomy, we call that containment gravity and it holds everything on the face of the earth down to the earth.

The earth was 'empty' because God was yet to populate it as He desired. The whole earth was still under water and land had to be raised to populate the earth. This mention of the earth being empty is simply God reporting the state of things as He progressed through His grand plan for the earth and the universe. Here is what God said in Isaiah:

Darkness was over the surface of the water because God stirred up enormous clouds of moisture from the water in cooling the molten earth that lies under the water; and God had not brought in light yet. Here is God saying it in Job:

[8] **"Who shut up the sea behind doors**
   when it burst forth from the womb,
[9] **when I made the clouds its garment**
   and wrapped it in thick darkness,

¹⁰ when I fixed limits for it
  and set its doors and bars in place,
¹¹ when I said, 'This far you may come and no farther;
  here is where your proud waves halt'? *(Job 38:8-11).*

That is why God said in Isaiah: **⁷ <u>I form the light</u> <u>and create darkness</u>, I bring prosperity and create disaster; I, the Lᴏʀᴅ, do all these things."** *(Isaiah 45:7).* Darkness rose from the quenching of the massive molten 'blob', so thick it resulted in pitch darkness over the water. And the Spirit of God was over the water.

And when God called for the light in Genesis 1:3-5 and the light showed through His Son Jesus Christ, God separated that Light from the already prevailing darkness to create not only day and night but also to separate darkness—that of the heart that is yet to come upon the earth—from the light that is Jesus Christ that had just descended upon the earth.

Therefore, the earth being formless, empty and dark as described in Genesis 1:2 was not a sign of imperfection; or deformation resulting from Satan 'throwing the wrench into the works' as some have previously suggested.

The only shock here is that mankind, in its haste, to slam God and the Bible denied itself the opportunity to avoid the craziness the devil brought into human lives and have since been paying dearly for our disobedience of God.

"For the message of the cross is foolishness to those who are perishing, but to us who are being saved it is the power of God. ¹⁹ For it is written:

"I will destroy the wisdom of the wise;
  the intelligence of the intelligent I will frustrate."[c]

²⁰ Where is the wise person? Where is the teacher of the law? Where is the philosopher of this age? Has not God made foolish the wisdom of the world? ²¹ <u>*For since in the wisdom of God the world through its wisdom did not know him, God was pleased through the foolishness of what was preached to save those who believe.*</u> *²² Jews demand signs and Greeks look for wisdom, ²³ but we preach Christ crucified: a stumbling block to Jews and foolishness to Gentiles, ²⁴ but to those whom God has called, both Jews and Greeks, Christ the power of God and the wisdom of God. ²⁵ For the foolishness of God is wiser than human wisdom, and the weakness of God is stronger than human strength."* *(1 Corinthians 1:18-25).*

The original light of Day One was not extinguished for the set of lights that were created on Day 4 to go into effect. Rather, at God's second command for light, Genesis 1:14-19, a cataclysmic event that changed everything took place. But before this event, God performed another huge creation—Genesis 1:6-8—that preceded and aided the cataclysmic event.

God commanded for a huge expanse to separate waters from waters, and this resulted in the creation of space. Here is the passage from the Bible: *"And God said, "Let there be an expanse between the waters to separate water from water." ⁷ So God made the expanse and separated the water under the expanse from the water above it. And it was so. ⁸ God called the expanse "sky." And there was evening, and there was morning—the second day."* *(Genesis 1:6-8).*

Here is a reminder to the reader: It is God that we are talking about here. He is Almighty and all-knowing and does whatever He chooses to do. Nothing is too big for Him to think, plan and do. Remember that the passage says: *"And God said, "Let there be an expanse between the waters to separate water from water." ⁷ So God made the expanse and separated the water under the expanse from the water above it. And it was so." (Genesis 1:6-7).*

The expanse that God made to separate the water under the expanse and the water above the expanse is 'space' as we know it today: The space in its sprawling stretches is used by God 'to separate water from water.' Therefore beyond all the starry hosts—that we gaze at and marvel at the power of God—lies a huge deep 'blanket' of water that completely covers the perimeter of space and bounds it. And this blanket of water constituted the farther bounds and control for the cataclysmic event of Genesis 1:14-19.

When you separate water from water in continuous and unbroken columns—spheres in the case of the waters of the creation—you create vacuum. We do the same thing today using the aspirators in the laboratories across our learning institutions and industries.

So this vacuum was created by God for the very next step in His creation—which is Genesis 1:14-19—"***And God said, "Let there be lights in the expanse of the sky to separate the day from the night, and let them serve as signs to mark sacred times, and days and years, [15] and let them be lights in the expanse of the sky to give light on the earth." And it was so. [16] God made two great lights— the greater light to govern the day and the lesser light to govern the night. He also made the stars. [17] God set them in the expanse of the sky to give light on the earth, [18] to govern the day and the night, and to separate light from darkness. And God saw that it was good. [19] And there was evening, and there was morning—the fourth day."***

With everything thus set to go, at God's second command, 'Let there be light,' that original light that came on Day 1 cataclysmically sent flaming balls of fires shuttling through space in every direction, propelled farther and farther away from the earth by the vacuum that was created when God created the space in Genesis 1:6-8.

In essence, Jesus Christ the original light of the earth for Day 1 through Day 3 transformed in nanoseconds into unbelievably expansive flaming balls of fire and filled the space God had just created in Genesis 1:6-8. This is why the Bible says in the Book of Ephesians: *"There is one body and one Spirit, just as you were called to one hope when you were called; ⁵ one Lord, one faith, one baptism; ⁶ one God and Father of all, who is over all and through all and in all.*

⁷ But to each one of us grace has been given as Christ apportioned it. ⁸ This is why it[ᵃ] says:

"When he ascended on high,
  he took many captives
  and gave gifts to his people."[ᵇ]

⁹ (What does "he ascended" mean except that he also descended to the lower, earthly regions[ᶜ]? ¹⁰ He who descended is the very one who ascended higher than all the heavens, in order to fill the whole universe.)" (Ephesians 4:4-10).

  "He who descended is the very one who ascended higher than all the heavens, in order to fill the whole universe." (Ephesians 4:4-10): In Genesis 1:14-19 Jesus Christ *"ascended higher than all the heavens, in order to fill the whole universe."*. And in after He was crucified, died and was buried in the tomb belonging to Joseph of Arimathea, Jesus Christ *"descended to the lower, earthly regions"* where He defeated the power of darkness once and for all and then rose three days later and ascended into heaven and sat the right hand of God the Father.

  It is important to note that at creation, Jesus Christ was the original light that graced the surface of the earth and He did that for three days. Why was it necessary for Christ to shine on one half of the earth for each of the three days and not all of the face of the earth? God in Genesis One continue to talk about separating the light from the darkness. That was an important distinction He made throughout.

The light and darkness He was referring to in these passages is not simply day and night but also good and evil. That was a great part of God's consideration right from the start; and He made light and darkness coexist on earth for those three days when His own beloved Son was the light that shined on earth.

God allowed darkness to survive because He knew that Lucifer would go to the dark side and as such, God prepared for that event ahead of time, by accommodating darkness in His grand design. Yes! Living things grew acclimatized to resting and refreshing their life systems at night. That was the purpose of the night, and God specifically called that out in His plan.

But there is a 'darkness' greater than the night; and that darkness was a concern to God more than anything else. That is the darkness of the heart which Satan started and would exploit to the fullest among mankind. And Adam and Eve would later fall into this darkness at the Garden of Eden; nudged on by Satan.

So God factored this impending darkness into His design and made plans and provisions, not only to contain it, but also to stamp it out forever at the right time. This darkness is death. God will be extending His Spirit to man because He would rear Him as His son. He is reluctant to destroy something that stems from His and is continually sustained by Him.

The entire human history is a window of time God given to humanity to experience God's infinite love. It is also the how long God has allowed humanity to repent from its sins and wickedness and return to God with Love and thankfulness. So God made provisions to contain the darkness before the darkness comes into the world — knowing for sure that it would come.

Chapter 4

Why Did God—the Light—Allow Darkness On The Earth?

Darkness was over the surface of the water because God stirred up enormous clouds of moisture from the water in cooling the molten earth that lies under the water; and God had not brought in light yet. Here is God saying it in Job:

[8] *"Who shut up the sea behind doors*
    when it burst forth from the womb,
[9] *when I made the clouds its garment*
    and wrapped it in thick darkness,
[10] *when I fixed limits for it*
    and set its doors and bars in place,
[11] *when I said, 'This far you may come and no farther;*
    here is where your proud waves halt'? (Job 38:8-11).

That is why God said in Isaiah: [7] *I form the light and create darkness, I bring prosperity and create disaster; I, the LORD, do all these things."* (Isaiah 45:7). Darkness rose from the quenching of the massive molten 'blob', so thick it resulted in pitch darkness over the water. And the Spirit of God was over the water.

Jesus Christ was the original light on the earth on Day 1 of the creation, and had the power to completely devastate and annihilate this darkness; but He was made to wait until God the Father says it is time. Jesus Christ obeys His Father passionately, and would not attempt anything until His father says so. So He allowed darkness to occupy half of the earth in the beginning, honoring His Father's wish and following His grand design.

At the dawn of time, Jesus Christ spent three days on earth as the light of the earth; yet He allowed darkness to remain on half of the earth every one of the three days. Jesus Christ came into the earth to route darkness and put it on the run. Darkness receded as soon as He showed up in Genesis 1:3-5 and God created a boundary between Jesus Christ the light of the world and darkness which is wickedness and evil. That is what God was referring to in the following passage:

"Have you ever given orders to the morning,
or shown the dawn its place,
13 that it might take the earth by the edges
and shake the wicked out of it?
14 The earth takes shape like clay under a seal;
its features stand out like those of a garment.
15 The wicked are denied their light,
and their upraised arm is broken." (Job 38:12-15).

16 "Have you journeyed to the springs of the sea
or walked in the recesses of the deep?
17 Have the gates of death been shown to you?
Have you seen the gates of the deepest darkness?" (Job 38:16-17).

God did not permit the original light on earth—Jesus Christ—to overcome the entire darkness, because He had plan to one day in the future send His Son back to the earth to finish that work and rout the evil one out in the process. And just over two thousand years ago, Jesus Christ returned to the earth as a man to save mankind. The Bible says

"Since the children have flesh and blood, he too shared in their humanity so that by his death he might break the power of him who holds the power of death—that is, the devil— 15 and free those who all their lives were held in slavery by their fear of death. (Hebrews 2:14-15).

For surely it is not angels he helps, but Abraham's descendants. [17] For this reason he had to be made like them,[k] fully human in every way, in order that he might become a merciful and faithful high priest in service to God, and that he might make atonement for the sins of the people. [18] Because he himself suffered when he was tempted, he is able to help those who are being tempted." (Hebrews 2:16-18).

At the end of His ministry on the earth, He spent another three days under the earth, and by so doing, completely overcame the power of darkness and received the crown from His Father for efficiently carrying out that task which had long been in the planning. He triumphed over the dark forces at work on the planet earth. He overcame death. Here is the passage from the Bible about the three day:

"He answered, "A wicked and adulterous generation asks for a sign! But none will be given it except the sign of the prophet Jonah. [40] For as Jonah was three days and three nights in the belly of a huge fish, so the Son of Man will be three days and three nights in the heart of the earth." *(Matthew 12:39-40).*

And He promises that He will be coming back to the earth one final time to secure His final victory over the forces of darkness that have dominated the earth since Satan deceived man into giving up the dominion of it. And that return will be a time of reckoning; not just for Satan and his angels but for men and women who like the devil chose to follow darkness. And people all over the world are looking forward to that event; some to receive their salvation and others to see if the prophecy would actually come true.

And here is what Apostle Peter said about that darkness:

"But there were also false prophets among the people, just as there will be false teachers among you. They will secretly introduce destructive heresies, even denying the sovereign Lord who bought them—bringing swift destruction on themselves. ² Many will follow their depraved conduct and will bring the way of truth into disrepute. ³ In their greed these teachers will exploit you with fabricated stories. Their condemnation has long been hanging over them, and their destruction has not been sleeping.

⁴ For if God did not spare angels when they sinned, but sent them to hell,[a] <u>putting them in chains of darkness</u>[b] to be held for judgment; ⁵ if he did not spare the ancient world when he brought the flood on its ungodly people, but protected Noah, a preacher of righteousness, and seven others; ⁶ if he condemned the cities of Sodom and Gomorrah by burning them to ashes, and made them an example of what is going to happen to the ungodly; ⁷ and if he rescued Lot, a righteous man, who was distressed by the depraved conduct of the lawless ⁸ (for that righteous man, living among them day after day, was tormented in his righteous soul by the lawless deeds he saw and heard)— ⁹ if this is so, then the Lord knows how to rescue the godly from trials and to hold the unrighteous for punishment on the day of judgment. ¹⁰ This is especially true of those who follow the corrupt desire of the flesh[c] and despise authority.

Bold and arrogant, they are not afraid to heap abuse on celestial beings; ¹¹ yet even angels, although they are stronger and more powerful, do not heap abuse on such beings when bringing judgment on them from[d] the Lord. ¹² But these people blaspheme in matters they do not understand. They are like unreasoning animals, creatures of instinct, born only to be caught and destroyed, and like animals they too will perish.

¹³ They will be paid back with harm for the harm they have done. Their idea of pleasure is to carouse in broad daylight. They are blots and blemishes, reveling in their pleasures while they feast with you. ¹⁴ With eyes full of adultery, they never stop sinning; they seduce the unstable; they are experts in greed—an accursed brood! ¹⁵ They have left the straight way and wandered off to follow the way of Balaam son of Bezer, who loved the wages of wickedness. ¹⁶ But he was rebuked for his wrongdoing by a donkey—an animal without speech—who spoke with a human voice and restrained the prophet's madness.

¹⁷ These people are springs without water and mists driven by a storm. <u>Blackest darkness is reserved for them.</u> ¹⁸ For they mouth empty, boastful words and, by appealing to the lustful desires of the flesh, they entice people who are just escaping from those who live in error. ¹⁹ They promise them freedom, while they themselves are slaves of depravity—for "people are slaves to whatever has mastered them." ²⁰ If they have escaped the corruption of the world by knowing our Lord and Savior Jesus Christ and are again entangled in it and are overcome, they are worse off at the end than they were at the beginning. ²¹ It would have been better for them not to have known the way of righteousness, than to have known it and then to turn their backs on the sacred command that was passed on to them. ²² Of them the proverbs are true: "A dog returns to its vomit," and, "A sow that is washed returns to her wallowing in the mud." (2 Peter 2:1-22).

So darkness was over the surface of the deep because there was no light on the earth until God commanded light to invade the darkness. And when the light came in, darkness receded to one side of the earth, not only to give cover to the night but also to symbolize darkness of the heart that would ultimately descend onto the earth.

God laid it before us in black and white within the first few verses in the Bible that the earth was round but nobody picked it up from God's account of creation. The so-called intellectuals of the world were in so much a hurry to discredit God and trample the Bible under their feet that they dismissed God's account of creation in the Bible and sought ways to disprove God and glorify themselves instead.

The Bible says: *"And God said, "Let there be light," and there was light. ⁴ God saw that the light was good, and he separated the light from the darkness. ⁵ God called the light "day," and the darkness he called "night." And there was evening, and there was morning—the first day."* (Genesis 1:3-5).

Here is what God said in Isaiah about His creation in Genesis One:

⁵ I am the Lᴏʀᴅ, and there is no other;
 apart from me there is no God.
I will strengthen you,
 though you have not acknowledged me,
⁶ so that from the rising of the sun
 to the place of its setting
people may know there is none besides me.
 I am the Lᴏʀᴅ, and there is no other.
⁷ I form the light and create darkness,
 I bring prosperity and create disaster;
 I, the Lᴏʀᴅ, do all these things. (Isaiah 45:5-7).

⁸ "You heavens above, rain down my righteousness;
 let the clouds shower it down.
Let the earth open wide,
 let salvation spring up,
let righteousness flourish with it;
 I, the Lᴏʀᴅ, have created it." (Isaiah 45:8).

"It is I who made the earth
 and created mankind on it.

__My own hands stretched out the heavens;__
__   I marshaled their starry hosts.__" (Isaiah 45:12).

"__My own hand laid the foundations of the earth,__
__   and my right hand spread out the heavens;__
__when I summon them,__
__   they all stand up together.__" (Isaiah 48:13).

And here is what God said in other passages from the Bible concerning God being the light:

"This is the message we have heard from him and declare to you: __God is light__; in him there is no darkness at all." (1 John 1:5).

"When Jesus spoke again to the people, he said, '__I am the light of the world__. Whoever follows me will never walk in darkness, but will have the light of life.'" (John 14:5-7).

"__The sun will no more be your light by day, nor will the brightness of the moon shine on you, for the Lord will be your everlasting light__, and your God will be your glory." (Isaiah 60:19).

"__Your sun will never set again, and your moon will wane no more; the Lord will be your everlasting light__, and your days of sorrow will end." (Isaiah 60:20).

"__Your sun will never set again, and your moon will wane no more; the Lord will be your everlasting light__, and your days of sorrow will end." (Matthew 24:29).

"__There will be no more night. They will not need the light of a lamp or the light of the sun, for the Lord God will give them light__." (Revelation 22:5).

God is the source of light and had imparted light on all known sources of light in the universe like the quasi, the stars, the sun and the moon as part of His creation design so they could serve the purposes He intended them to serve. Nobody can give something he does not have. So God gives light because He already has light in Him, and that is what the preceding passages are alluding to.

When God commanded for light to dawn on the newly formed earth, and light appeared on the earth, we immediately assume that the light came from the sun since the sun is and has been the source of light on earth since man was brought onto the earth. But that was an incorrect assumption. God did something spectacular in Genesis 1:3-5.

In Genesis 1:3-5, when God commanded: **"Let there be light,"** light came upon the surface of the earth. But that light was not from the sun: That light that first graced the face of the earth came directly from within God Almighty Himself **"and there was light. [4] God saw that the light was good, and he separated the light from the darkness. [5] God called the light "day," and the darkness he called "night." And there was evening, and there was morning—the first day."** (Genesis 1:3-5).

Chapter 5

The Big Bang — Jesus Christ Birthed the Universe!

It is important to note that God creating space before Christ's cataclysmic transformation that filled the entire universe is extremely essential—giving the extreme nature of the transformation. God had just announced the kickoff of space and had just put all powers and principalities on notice about His intent. He created the void to catch the 'wild'—yet controlled— and expansive spread that was about to happen.

On the scientific side, the unfathomable amount of energy that was dispersed in one short instance to create the universe could have incinerated the recently formed earth and vaporize the deluge of water that protected it and leave nothing at the end, just like in a bomb calorimeter. That is the extent of the power of God that was at display in this event.

So God had His Holy Spirit stand guard over the earth and the water covering it. Then God stretched the void that He put in-between the waters to divide the waters, creating an expansive vacuum; not only to absorb the energy released in the cataclysmic dispersion of the fireballs but also to pull them away from the earth and the water below the void as quickly as possible, to the far reaches of the space He had created.

So contrary to what science predicts today, the earth did not precipitate out of an exploding universe; but according to our Bible, the universe was dispersed from around the earth by God the Father, God the Son and God the Holy Spirit. Also, the earth did not come into existence by chance, it was very thoughtfully designed and articulated, and then expertly formed with love to house you and I and all of mankind. And this is why the bible says: ***"I praise you because <u>I am fearfully and wonderfully made</u>; your works are wonderful, I know that full well."*** *(Psalm 139:14).*

And the universe is not filled with millions of earthlike planets. Our earth is indeed the center of the universe. It all started on earth which God created before any other part of our fading universe was created. Our Bible says so and we have had the occasion to uncover more truths that were hidden in plain sight on the very first page of our great Bible. That is the power of God. That is the discernment of the Holy Spirit and the gift of our Lord Jesus Christ.

Maybe now we can all channel our mental energies in the right direction and have our Lord Jesus Christ lead us to more great truths so we can grow our faiths in Him to maturity and have the life we are all promised to have on this earth and in into eternity.

Just as the moon—as a lesser light to the sun and a reflector of the sun's light—is set in space as a sign for us to see; and the sun and all the starry hosts that are in space are an agglomeration of lesser lights to the original light of creation—Jesus Christ the Son of God; the waters in the clouds—in the sky within the stratosphere of the earth—is also set above the earth as a sign to humanity, symbolizing a much larger body of water beyond what we know as space today. And that body of water is referred to in Genesis 1:6-8 as the water above the expanse.

Many have long belittled the power of Genesis as the true creation account because they were not looking at the information with discernment which can only come from the Spirit of God. They were simply scouring the Book as if they were looking into a text book or literature, and were denied the information contained in that Book of documentation of the grandest experiments that had ever been performed in all of the universe and throughout all the ages. And there would be none quite like it again.

Science has dismissed Genesis as meaningless because science did not realize that much information on the Genesis account of creation is tucked away from humanity and placed out of the human reach forever, because God knew who and what He made in man: a diabolic, scheming and conniving soul that seeks after self-aggrandizement more than anything else; yet capable of love and kindness and heartwarming fellowship.

Jesus Christ is in every atom of everything in the universe. That is the grand purpose of creation in Genesis 1:14-19. That gives Jesus Christ supremacy over everything in the universe.

"The Son is the image of the invisible God, the firstborn over all creation. [16] For in him all things were created: things in heaven and on earth, visible and invisible, whether thrones or powers or rulers or authorities; all things have been created through him and for him. [17] He is before all things, and in him all things hold together. [18] And he is the head of the body, the church; he is the beginning and the firstborn from among the dead, so that in everything he might have the supremacy. [19] For God was pleased to have all his fullness dwell in him, [20] and through him to reconcile to himself all things, whether things on earth or things in heaven, by making peace through his blood, shed on the cross.

21 Once you were alienated from God and were enemies in your minds because of[g] your evil behavior. 22 But now he has reconciled you by Christ's physical body through death to present you holy in his sight, without blemish and free from accusation— 23 <u>if you continue in your faith, established and firm, and do not move from the hope held out in the gospel</u>. This is the gospel that you heard and that has been proclaimed to every creature under heaven, and of which I, Paul, have become a servant." (Colossians 1:15-23).

This grand purpose of creation—about Jesus Christ being in every atom of all things created—is why Jesus says in the Gospel of John: *"I am the true vine, and my Father is the gardener. 2 <u>He cuts off every branch in me that bears no fruit, while every branch that does bear fruit he prunes[a] so that it will be even more fruitful</u>. 3 You are already clean because of the word I have spoken to you. 4 Remain in me, as I also remain in you. No branch can bear fruit by itself; it must remain in the vine. Neither can you bear fruit unless you remain in me.*

5 "I am the vine; you are the branches. If you remain in me and I in you, you will bear much fruit; apart from me you can do nothing. 6 If you do not remain in me, you are like a branch that is thrown away and withers; such branches are picked up, thrown into the fire and burned. 7 If you remain in me and my words remain in you, ask whatever you wish, and it will be done for you. 8 This is to my Father's glory, that you bear much fruit, showing yourselves to be my disciples.

9 "As the Father has loved me, so have I loved you. Now remain in my love. 10 If you keep my commands, you will remain in my love, just as I have kept my Father's commands and remain in his love. 11 I have told you this so that my joy may be in you and that your joy may be complete. 12 My command is this: Love each other as I have loved you. 13 Greater love has no one than this: to lay down one's life for one's friends. 14 You are my friends if you do what I command. [15] I no longer call you servants, because a servant does not know his master's business. Instead, I have called you friends, for everything that I learned from my Father I have made known to you. [16] You did not choose me, but I chose you and appointed you so that you might go and bear fruit—fruit that will last—and so that whatever you ask in my name the Father will give you. [17] This is my command: Love each other." John15:1-17).

"He cuts off every branch in me that bears no fruit, while every branch that does bear fruit he prunes[a] so that it will be even more fruitful." (John 15:2): You heard it. Jesus Christ is telling us that both the good and the bad are in him because He is the very life in every man and woman on the surface of the earth.

And those who are not obedient to Him are branches in Him that will be cut off of Him by God the Father and thrown into the fire and burned. And those who obey Him are His friends and remain in Him because they are the branches in Him which God the Father will prune so that they will be even more fruitful.

In other words, God became the light for the new earth that first day, and continued to be the light for the second and the third day on the earth—that is up to Genesis 1:14-19. Then, God commanded again: **"Let there be lights in the firmament of the heaven to divide the day from the night; and let them be for signs, and for seasons, and for days, and years [15] And let them be for lights in the firmament of the heaven to give light upon the earth, and it was so."** *(Genesis 1:14-15).*

[16] *"God made two great lights—the greater light to govern the day and the lesser light to govern the night. He also made the stars. [17] God set them in the expanse of the sky to give light on the earth, [18] to govern the day and the night, and to separate light from darkness. And God saw*

that it was good. [19] And there was evening, and there was morning—the fourth day." (Genesis 1:16-19).

At this second command of God for light, the sun, the moon and the stars were made by God to give light to the earth. It is important to note that the underlined sections of the above passage said that these lights were designed "***to give light upon the earth***", in addition to various other things God designed them to accomplish.

Why would God design a new light on day four *to give light upon the earth* when He had already brought light to the earth on the first day? Because the light from day one came from a different source than the light from day four; and God substituted the light from day one with the light from day 4!

It is also very important to note that God was careful to tell us that the new lights will also be for signs: **"*Let there be lights in the firmament of the heaven to divide the day from the night; and let them be for signs.*"** God substituted the first light He cast on the earth with a set of lights, all of which work together to serve God's purposes on earth, including conveying God's signs to all mankind. This confirms what Apostle Paul told us in the Book of Romans:

[18] "The wrath of God is being revealed from heaven against all the godlessness and wickedness of people, who suppress the truth by their wickedness, [19] since what may be known about God is plain to them, because God has made it plain to them. [20] For since the creation of the world God's invisible qualities—his eternal power and divine nature—have been clearly seen, being understood from what has been made, so that people are without excuse." (Romans 1:18-20).

[21] "For although they knew God, they neither glorified him as God nor gave thanks to him, but their thinking became futile and their foolish hearts were darkened. [22] Although

they claimed to be wise, they became fools [23] and exchanged the glory of the immortal God for images made to look like a mortal human being and birds and animals and reptiles." *(Romans 1:21-23).*

It is this aspect of these celestial bodies—being designed to give signs to the world—that got many ancient people off track, causing them to worship these bodies and many other created things, instead of seeking the true God. The ancient philosophers also dedicated their careers trying to decipher these signs and wonders of God; and many times misinterpreted them because they were not looking for God.

Rather, they easily settled for hasty assumptions and erroneous conclusions. Astrology, divination, and contacting the spirit of the dead were all such misdirected human pursuits as mankind attempted to understand the signs and wonders our great God leaves in and around these celestial bodies.

And while the ancient people got carried away in their efforts to decipher the signs and wonders that God has created in and around these celestial bodies, science arose and decided to rewrite everything that God Himself wrote. Science concluded that the celestial bodies hold no signs from God. And that God is a myth and never existed.

Scientists began to propose that the heavens hold no mystery from God' but that it is rather a new frontier for the all-mighty mankind to attack and subdue. Some are even suggesting that if God exists, we would finally rout him out. Here is an internet excerpt about Stephen Hawking's comments about God:

Science, truth and beauty: Hawking's answers

What is the value in knowing "Why are we here?"

115

The universe is governed by science. But <u>science tells us that we can't solve the equations, directly in the abstract. We need to use the effective theory of Darwinian natural selection of those societies most likely to survive. We assign them higher value.</u>

You've said there is no reason to invoke God to light the blue touchpaper. Is our existence all down to luck?

Science predicts that many different kinds of universe will be spontaneously created out of nothing. It is a matter of chance which we are in.

So here we are. What should we do?

We should seek the greatest value of our action.

You had a health scare and spent time in hospital in 2009. What, if anything, do you fear about death?

I have lived with the prospect of an early death for the last 49 years. I'm not afraid of death, but I'm in no hurry to die. I have so much I want to do first. I regard the brain as a computer which will stop working when its components fail. <u>There is no heaven or afterlife for broken down computers; that is a fairy story for people afraid of the dark</u>.

What are the things you find most beautiful in science?

Science is beautiful when it makes simple explanations of phenomena or connections between different observations. Examples include the double helix in biology, and the fundamental equations of physics." (THIS IS THE END OF THE INTERVIEW)

"The physicist's remarks draw a stark line between the use of God as a metaphor and the belief in an omniscient creator whose hands guide the workings of the cosmos." *(Comment from Stephen Hawking's interviewer).*

"In his bestselling 1988 book, A Brief History of Time, <u>Hawking drew on the device so beloved of Einstein, when he described what it would mean for scientists to develop a "theory of everything" – a set of equations that described every particle and force in the entire universe.</u>

"It would be the ultimate triumph of human reason – for then we should know the mind of God," he wrote". *(Comment from Stephen Hawking's interviewer).*

Pay attention to the underlined sections of this excerpt: First, to believe that there is God and that there is heaven *is a fairy story for people afraid of the dark.* Yet Mr. Hawking admitted that **"the universe is governed by science. But science tells us that we can't solve the equations, directly in the abstract."** So to get around their dilemma as the smarted people in the world of science, he said: **"We need to use the effective theory of Darwinian natural selection of those societies most likely to survive. We assign them higher value."**

Man has become too smart that, first, he dismisses the facts about the existence of God and heaven as being 'afraid of the dark'. And to prove his point about the non-existence of God, his best effort would be to borrow from the Theory of Evolution and 'assign higher value' to "those societies most likely to survive'. What qualifies any human being to assign any value whatsoever to any group of mysterious and unknown entities?

Well, if anyone says there is no God, I suspect that automatically qualifies that person as god—yes, god—because nobody in the world, and nothing in the entire universe, could ascend to the position of God. Unfortunately this kind of postulation from the distinguished scientist from England does not convince me as much as the Bible does. I am sticking with the Bible and I hope the rest of the world will do the same!

Now back to the revelation of Genesis 1:3-5 and Genesis 1:14-19. By making this switch from the original light—Light from God from Dai 1 to Day 3—to the replacement lights—Light from Day 4 up until the present time—), God tucked away one mystery for mankind to discover and appreciate the limitless wisdom of God.

God promises the following in the last chapter of the Book of Revelation about the saints in the New Jerusalem that came down to the earth: ***"There will be no more night. They will not need the light of a lamp or the light of the sun, for the Lord God will give them light. And they will reign for ever and ever"*** *(Revelation 22:5).* When He does that, it would not be the first time He did it. He started the earth without the aid of the sun, the moon and the stars and

He will end the current state of the earth without the aid of the sun, the moon and the stars. He Himself was the original light that graced the face of the earth and He Himself will be the light that graces the face of the New Earth once He extinguishes the lights of the sun, the moon and the stars. He will end it all the same way He started it all.

And this is the reason why God tells us that He makes known the end from the beginning. Here is the passage from the Bible: "***I make known the end from the beginning****, from ancient times, what is still to come. I say, 'My purpose will stand, and I will do all that I please.'"* *(Isaiah 46:10).* To kick things off on the new planet He had just created and was still forming, God become its light.

And once God introduce life to the earth, He designed the sun to become the permanent source of light that is needed by all living things on the earth, so they could thrive and multiply. God created the sun, the moon and the stars to shine their light upon the earth so that life on the planet earth could thrive: the sun provides the necessary light to the earth and everything living in it; and God continues to maintain His Spirit in man, and life in other living things.

First God created water to cover the entire surface of the earth and the Bible tells us that at this point, *"the earth was formless and empty, darkness was over the surface of the deep, and **the Spirit of God was hovering**

over the waters. *"(Genesis 1:2).* Water and the Spirit of God in communion with one another! Coincidence! Not at all! Water symbolizes the Spirit of God, and here at the very beginning of the earth the Spirit of God was over the waters, suggesting that water got its characteristics from the Spirit of God. That might explain why water has such a powerful effect on our lives; and plays extremely vital roles in the supporting life.

Water is the medium for the blood; and the Bible tells us that life is in the blood. And that the life in man is the spirit of man and the Breath of the Almighty God. Therefore the spirit of man—which is the life in man—is intricately intertwined with the water in the blood. In virtually all circumstances where the Spirit of God is mentioned in the Bible, the Spirit of God is described as 'being poured" hinting of a fluid-like existence.

And the Bible also tells us that it is the spirit of man that gives man understanding. So if man's spirit is in man's blood and the blood is dispersed in water, then water is not only vital in man's nutrition, it is also vital in man's intellect; not just to help maintain the nutrition of the brain, the brain's electrolyte and electrical balance and overall mental and emotional health of man, but also the soul's spiritual needs and operations.

Water is used in the holy baptism to wash away the sinful nature and allow the Holy Spirit to come into a believer of Jesus Christ. Pontius Pilate washed his hands and indicated to the Jews that he is absolving himself from all blames for sending Jesus Christ to the cross. And he is not alone in using water to wash off guilt. That is still practiced in some cultures today.

Without water life will simply cease to exist. The same is true of light and that is why God created light on the earth—not only to maintain life but to mark day and night. God even made the moon to take light from the sun and beam it to the dark half of the earth and called it night.

Jesus Christ was the singular source of light on the earth for the first three days and provided the earth with another singular but very powerful source of light as the sun. And He made the sun different from all the other stars in the universe and set them much farther away into space to mesmerize our senses.

The Spirit of God being over the water that covered the surface of the newly formed earth from the moment the earth was formed was an indication for how special God designed the earth to be. It goes to show that God really put in so much of Himself in designing and forming this one planet, because He intended to put His most precious creation—mankind—on it.

God's Spirit was all over the water. And from John 1:1-5, we know that Jesus Christ the Son of God was there, too, both as the spoken word of God and the light that came forth when God commanded for light: **_"In the beginning was the Word, and the Word was with God, and the Word was God. [2] He was with God in the beginning. [3] Through him all things were made; without him nothing was made that has been made. [4] In him was life, and that life was the light of all mankind. [5] The light shines in the darkness, and the darkness has not overcome it."_** _(John 1:1-5)._

God made Himself the first light that shined on the dark earth so He could bless every grain of sand on the earth, and everything the earth would contain, simply so the earth would be able to support mankind. The passage from John one said that in Jesus Christ was life and that life was the light of all mankind. John is saying here that Jesus Christ is the life that is in man which is the spirit of man and which both sustains the man and enlightens the man.

John was describing the very beginning of the earth here; just as it is written in Genesis One: ***"The light shines in the darkness, and the darkness has not overcome it."*** This passage is saying that when God commanded there to be light and the light (Jesus Christ) came forth, that the light shined in the darkness that engulfed the entire earth and yet the darkness did not overcome the light (Jesus Christ), in spite of the enormity of the darkness.

The passage is describing the unfathomable power of Jesus Christ in sufficiently and reliably serving the whole earth as its source of light. And according to Genesis 1:3-5 Jesus Christ provided light for the whole earth from Day 1 to day three. And on the fourth day, God commanded again for lights and this time to be set in space from which they are beamed to the young earth.

And by serving as light to the world, together with His Father, Jesus Christ became the originator and sustainer of life on earth: originator, because He passed the life in Him on to things the living things He created on the earth; and sustainer, because of His Spirit that continues to flourish in man and because He left in His stead the sun to continue to fuel life on the earth.

And to dispel all arguments that what God created in Genesis 1:3-5 and what He created in Genesis 1:14-19 were one and the same, rather than two disparate lights for the same purpose, God in His narrative set each of these two light creations on the day He created it. Genesis 1:3-5 happened on the very first day of creation while Genesis 1:14-19 happened on the fourth day of creation. And the details about each of the two creations are different as well.

In Genesis 1:3-5 God did not tell us the source and the location of the source of the light on the first day. But we know that for evening and morning to be possible throughout the earth, the earth being round, had to be rotated completely each day. So whatever conditions God set up on that first day with the light were simply carried on with the sum three days later.

The moon came with the sun on the fourth day and as such was no deployed from Day One as a satellite for the Day One's light. And the stars also came into existence of Day four with the sun and the moon. Notice that this order of the creation of these celestial bodies is in direct contradiction with what science and astronomy suggests today. Stars and the sun being in existence way before the earth and the other planets is critically essential for the scientists to be able to sell in their theory since it was plucked out of the abstract.

But your Bible tells you, among other things, that the Almighty God made the earth on Day One and on Day four, He made the sun, the moon and the stars and set them in space to give their lights. He made the sun and the moon greater light and lesser light.

To the sun, God gave enough light, heat and His vitality to power and give life to not just the earth but the other planets and satellites in the sun's solar system. And because God designed the sun to serve a greater number of celestial bodies and their horizons, He placed it much farther away from the earth and gave it greater intensity both in light and in heat and in God's vitality. Placing the sun any closer to the earth would scotch all life on earth.

To the moon, God gave reflective properties so it could reflect the light from the sun onto the planet earth—the portion of the earth that is facing away from the sun. And because God designed the moon to serve just the earth, He placed the moon in the vicinity of the earth so its soft light could cut through the earth's darkness.

Contrary to what the scientists suggested, the moon did not happen by chance, and the moon was not only intended to give light to the earth at night. The moon has a greater importance than that. The moon is placed so close to the earth by God so we can see it and pickup clues that God left for us about Himself and His love for humanity: As the light from the moon is only a reflection of the light from the sun; the lights from the sun, the stars and all the other sources of light in the universe are reflections of the original light that shined on the earth the first three days.

In other words, the light that comes from the sun, the stars and the quasi and all the other sources are reflections of the light that is Jesus Christ. The light that is Jesus Christ is so intense that God had to step it down immensely by porting it into trillions of stars and spread them across the universe. Then He parted a much smaller percentage of that original light onto the sun and positioned the sun much farther away from the earth for the planet earth to be able to withstand its intensity.

And the planets, Mercury and Jupiter serve to illustrate this unbearable intensity of the light that is Jesus Christ for all mankind. And the rest of the planets beyond the earth in the sun's solar system serve to demonstrate to us God's finesse in and His extreme tact in positioning the earth in the solar system.

The quasi, the trillions of stars and the sun, together are not large enough to contain the light that is Jesus Christ. That is why Genesis 1:14 says: **"And God said, Let there be lights in the firmament of the heaven to divide the day from the night; _and let them be for signs,_ and for seasons, and for days, and years."** *(Genesis 1:14)*. And these celestial bodies came into existence and each received only but a small fraction of the light that is Jesus Christ.

Between the creation of the two lights in Genesis 1:3-5 and Genesis 1:14-19, God did not mention that the light of Day One was somehow extinguish and the light of Day 4 took over. And in various passages in the Bible, we learn that Jesus was the light, is still the light and would forever be the light. And He guarantees us that at the very end, He will return and there will be no nights anymore and the services of the moon and the sun would no longer be required. He will remain with His saints and be their light forever.

Who should you believe, God or science and astronomy? Would you rather believe a man like yourself, who resorts to clever tactics like Stephen Hawking suggested: ***"The universe is governed by science. But science tells us that we can't solve the equations, directly in the abstract. We need to use the effective theory of Darwinian natural selection of those societies most likely to survive. We assign them higher value."*** *(Stephen Hawking).*

Or would you believe God who made you with love, sustains you with love, and made sure He gave you hope by giving you His words for your consumption and reflections, and as your offensive and defensive weapons in doing battle against the devil? A God that holds you in the highest place honor among all of His creations and did not hesitate to sacrifice His beloved Son so you may be redeemed from your sins and be purified and restored as if you have never sinned?

The choice is yours but that choice is also clear. You should obey God and accept His love and change your life to receive all His promises to those who have faith in Him. And the Bible says: ***"Now faith is confidence in what we hope for and assurance about what we do not*** *see. ² This is what the ancients were commended for. ³ By faith we understand that the universe was formed at God's command, so that what is seen was not made out of what was visible"* (Hebrews 11:1-3).

In Genesis 1:14-19 God told us that the sources of the lights on the fourth day were the sun and the moon and the stars. He also told us that they were set in space—***the expanse of the sky***—from where they cast their lights onto the earth, to create in addition to day and night, seasons, years and signs about God's Will for humanity. Here is the passage from Genesis:

And God said, "Let there be lights in the firmament of the heaven to divide the day from the night; and let them be for signs, and for seasons, and for days, and years ¹⁵ And let them be for lights in the firmament of the heaven to give light upon the earth, and it was so." (Genesis 1:14-15).

¹⁶ "God made two great lights—the greater light to govern the day and the lesser light to govern the night. He also made the stars. ¹⁷ <u>God set them in the expanse of the sky to give light on the earth</u>, ¹⁸ to govern the day and the night, and to separate light from darkness. And God saw that it was good. ¹⁹ And there was evening, and there was morning—the fourth day." (Genesis 1:16-19).

We deduced from Genesis 1:3-5—the very first Chapter of the Bible—that Jesus Christ was the first light that graced the face of the earth. And from Revelation Chapter 22—the very last Chapter of the Bible—God specifically told us that those who get into the New Jerusalem, *"will see his face, and his name will be on their foreheads. ⁵ <u>There will be no more night. They will not need the light of a lamp or the light of the sun, for the Lord God will give them light</u>. And they will reign for ever and ever."* (Revelation 22:5).

So, it will indeed be in the end as it was in the beginning: In the beginning, Jesus Christ was the light that shone on the planet earth before any man was created on the surface of the earth to contaminate the earth. And in the end when we are all washed of our sins, justified and sanctified, and enter the New Jerusalem, God once again will become the light that shines on the new heavens and the new earth.

The only difference between the beginning and the end on earth is that in the beginning, God was the light on the earth for just three days whereas in the end, He will be the light on the earth for everlasting.

Again, in the beginning, the sun, the moon and the stars first lent their lights to the earth three days after God mandated their services on the earth. And in the end, their services would be required no more because the original light will be restored on earth (the New Jerusalem that would come down to the earth from heaven); even becoming indigenous to it. What a great blessing for mankind.to share the same space with God, simply because we obeyed Him.

A good look at the following passages from the Bible speaks to the accuracy of this claim about God imparting light to everything in the universe that produces light. But most of Revelation Chapter 22 was placed here to provoke thoughts in readers who did not have the benefits of reading them from the Bible:

"__The stars of heaven and their constellations will not show their light. The rising sun will be darkened and the moon will not give its light.__" (Isaiah 13:10).

"__I form the light and create darkness__, I bring prosperity and create disaster; I, the Lord, do all these things." (Isaiah 45:7).

"Then the angel showed me the river of the water of life, as clear as crystal, flowing from the throne of God and of the Lamb [2] down the middle of the great street of the city.

On each side of the river stood the tree of life, bearing twelve crops of fruit, yielding its fruit every month. And the leaves of the tree are for the healing of the nations. ³ No longer will there be any curse. The throne of God and of the Lamb will be in the city, and his servants will serve him. ⁴ They will see his face, and his name will be on their foreheads. ⁵ <u>There will be no more night. They will not need the light of a lamp or the light of the sun, for the Lord God will give them light</u>. And they will reign for ever and ever.

⁶ The angel said to me, "These words are trustworthy and true. The Lord, the God who inspires the prophets, sent his angel to show his servants the things that must soon take place."

⁷ "Look, I am coming soon! Blessed is the one who keeps the words of the prophecy written in this scroll."

⁸ I, John, am the one who heard and saw these things. And when I had heard and seen them, I fell down to worship at the feet of the angel who had been showing them to me. ⁹ But he said to me, "Don't do that! I am a fellow servant with you and with your fellow prophets and with all who keep the words of this scroll. Worship God!"

¹⁰ Then he told me, 'Do not seal up the words of the prophecy of this scroll, because the time is near. ¹¹ Let the one who does wrong continue to do wrong; let the vile person continue to be vile; let the one who does right continue to do right; and let the holy person continue to be holy.'" (Revelation 22:1-11).

Nothing is more accurate than this account of the first day and night that ever existed on the planet earth. Because the earth is round and receives its light from the sun, only one half of the earth can see the light at a time while the other half is in darkness. And the Bible tells us that that is what God did the first time He let light filter into the horizon of the new planet (earth) that He just created.

It is mind boggling, if you think about it, that the Bible account left no vital information out, and still has unprecedented accuracy even in this jet age of science and astronomy. It is amazing that correctly applying all the proven scientific and astronomical facts we have today to this short account of creation in the Bible fits like hand in a glove; and even reveals more opportunities for further scientific exploration of this truth of God.

This also confirms the claims of the apostles that no word of God in the Bible is a creation of a prophet but rather God's very own words manifested through the prophet as the prophet is moved by the Spirit of God.

A quick look through the history of the church demonstrates that Christians have been reacting with uneasiness to pressures from the scientific world to 'update' the Scriptures so it would agree with scientific findings when a great percentage of these findings gained widespread acceptability simply because no one was able to come up with factual evidence to disprove the theory— just like in the case of the Theory of Evolution.

But that uneasiness is not at all necessary. We do not have to fight God's fight for Him. Our God is able and can and would win all His battles. All we are supposed to do is remain faithful to Him and obedient to His commands. We only need to show strong desires to gain knowledge so we may be able to refute some of the craziness that has been spread about the Almighty God. He will give us the knowledge and guarantee our victory over the enemies.

These scientists are more brazen that ever since these half-baked so-called truths have been touted by many for more than a century without any reprisal from society or God. Instead they have all become rich and famous and as such more fired up to come up with more insult to God. The attitude has become: 'If it continuous to work, why try to fix it'.

Whereas science and astronomy forge on to convince the world that the earth was the remains of a dead star that burned itself out, and through chance and time, became conducive for life to emerge from it and prosper on it, we should not feel threatened by their strong arguments and their so-called preponderance of evidence that supports their theory.

Their theory proposes that stars and the rest of the universe were formed billions of years before the earth was formed from a dead star. And some are even proposing that the life that exists on the earth first existed on Mars and came to the earth through a little chunk of Mars that detached from Mars and landed on earth. That is why the big governments of the world are funding scientific exploration of Mars for a possible sign of life so that science can claim victory over God's creation.

I hate to ruin their joy for them if and when they stumble on water or anything that hints at life elsewhere than just the planet earth. According to God's account in Genesis 1:6-8, there is water beyond space. Around the entire perimeter of space is a deluge of water far greater than what we have here on planet earth.

Those waters, coupled with the water that remains on the earth, were employed by God to draw a huge vacuum that became the present day space that we all know. So if we venture outside the space, we'll be swimming in deep oceans of water. I do not think anyone is encouraged to look that far before they can achieve their goal of finding anywhere other than the earth.

And we probably have failed to see these verses in Genesis One the way it was shown to me because we have conditioned ourselves to fit God within the confines of our human minds. That is not the true God! Everyone who has experienced God is left depleted and forever humbled because God is truly awe-inspiring!

To understand God's true power and capacity, you have to allow God to take you wherever He wants to take you and show you whatever He wants to show you. When He is done, the experience will leave you beaten and breathless. It's not you human wisdom that is required to understand God, it is the wisdom God will put in you as He takes you along. And anybody can experience God this way if he truly seeks it.

Science tries to convince you that the universe has been around for billions of years because the assumptions that the scientists made to make their theories even remotely convincing requires that long for the gradual natural changes they propose to become large enough to cause the kind of varieties we see around us; and secondly because for that unreasonable amount of time, asking them for proof seems unreasonable.

And by taking the argument from real and simple to complex and abstract, they get most regular people out of participation in the debate, thereby denying them the opportunity to actively seek the truth for themselves. And because every one of us has experienced the benefits that come from science and technologies—the improved services and products we all enjoy today—we readily succumb to the side of science. That is dangerous to not only those of us who hurriedly buy into the lies but more importantly to those others who would believe us because they trust our judgment—like our friends and families.

We need to be mindful that the Bible warms us of about such easy enticement because that is the devil's chief weapon. He uses that to keep seeking physical and here-and-now benefits over spiritual benefits and eternity. The Bible tells us that the world and everything in it belongs to the devil, and no one should take that advice lightly. We must critically weigh anything that science tells us against what the Bible tells us. Where science disagrees with the Bible, the truth is with the Bible. God must be first in our lives, no matter the temptation.

God, on the other hand, told us in Genesis that He actually created the earth before He created the sun, the moon and the stars to give light to the earth and serve as signs to the whole world. *(Genesis 1:1-19).* Our God is telling us that we are wonderfully and fearfully made and that He designed the universe for our purpose; and not us and our world for the purpose of universe. He is telling us that He put so much work in putting the earth together so that His most important creation—human beings—would be supported and protected.

But science disagrees and insists that man, out of chance and circumstance, emerged on the earth, and has nobody to direct and care for him but himself. The stakeholders of science convince all of humanity that we are simply one of the animals that chance and time brought into the world; and that we only became as specialized as we are today through our own wits and wizardry—survival of the fittest.

And they convinced the world by unilaterally adopting the theory of evolution, in all schools and universities, as the truth of the origin of life and the universe. You are taught these theories from an early age that you become adjusted in that belief. And well into your working life, your job requires you to continue to hold on to these beliefs. And any attempts to break away from these beliefs usually result in losing the job you are in and being blacklisted for future lucrative jobs—since you need references from previous employment to get a new one.

If you do not buy into that argument why then should you buy into the one that claims that your Bible is fictitious and has no truth in it. If you are convinced that Genesis is a fiction, then Revelation and the rest of the Bible is also fictitious and has no use in your life. The Book of Genesis in the Bible is as real as your very existence is real; and in it God tells you the real purpose of your life.

If God had allowed Himself to become an object of economic exploitation to the point that the world desires and pursues, God and the Bible would have become the hottest commodity in the world throughout the ages. But because God is very much alive, unchangeable and in control, He remains committed to those who have faith in Him and who obey His commands; while at the same time monitoring the ruthless and those exploiting the innocent and the unsuspecting for personal gains, and putting stumbling blocks in their ways.

In light of this new revelation that God Himself became the light that shined on the earth for three days before relegating that responsibility to the sun, the moon and the stars, we have a lot to be thankful to God for. No one needs to have superior education or ability to understand abstract thinking to be able to have faith in God. He made it so simple for everyone to believe in Him and be saved. He even gave the world a huge number of people faithful to Him who are willingly to live in poverty and sacrifice their own comfort and even their lives just to save a single soul from the deceits of the devil and entanglement in worldly pursuits.

From everything the scientists have told the world, science is yet to show to the world a real life progression of these purported events that ultimately produced the earth and all the conditions that currently exist on it that made and continues to make life possible. But because everything they do is based on wealth and profit and backed by huge government budget, they could afford to continue to flex their muscle and trying to sweep all who believe in God into the ground.

But it will not continue that way forever. They can only do so for a season, and the time will come for the people of God to push back with the truth God makes available to them. The Israelites did it and got out of the bondage in Egypt. The church has also been promised the same victory over this corrupt and depraved world. The church has to unite and focus on being salt and light to the world to be able to unleash the power of God against God's enemies.

When the Genesis account was given to the world as God's account on the origin of the universe, mankind had neither the scientific and astronomical knowledge not the literary sophistication to project accurately that the earth was round and suspended on nothing.

Here in Genesis Chapter One, God told us that the earth is round and that is why darkness was separated from light as the day and the night. But we failed to grasp His revelation; and instead sought long and protracted methods to get to the information so we would endeavor to dispel the notion of the creator and claim for ourselves the glory that is due God.

Chapter 6

The Earth was Formless—All Part of Design, Not a Flaw.

In today's world, through Earth Science and Geology we know that the core of the earth is occupied by overheated molten lava that continues to churn around and build up pressure—venting itself every once in a while through volcanic eruption. The core of the earth did not get overheated mysteriously after the earth was formed. It has always been that way since its formation.

It becomes evident then that the water on the surface of the earth cooled the very top layer of the earth to whatever depth God desired and formed the sea beds. And from seismology we learn that the sea bed did not cool into one solid mass.

The sea bed cooled into huge intricate continental plates that move slightly away from or over one another to absorb built up pressures from the still churning molten core of the earth and helps maintain serenity on the surface of the earth. But when the movement of these continental plates is significant enough, it causes tremors that are felt on the surface of the earth and could trigger earthquakes.

And then the Bible says, "***And God said, Let the waters under the heaven be gathered together unto one place, and let the dry land appear: and it was so.***" Dense water vapor that resulted from the cooling of the sea bed, and was hovering over the water surface, was then pushed up into the expanse that became the sky and dispersed as clouds.

It is important to note that the moisture rose, from a smaller perimeter around the earth's surface, to a much larger perimeter, several miles perpendicular above the earth's surface. The moisture had a much larger area to cover when it rose, so it dispersed, and as a result, it could not immediately result in a rain.

Cataclysmic volcanic eruption brought molten lava through the standing water to the surface of the water. The lava cooled quickly from the massive amount of the water it displaced; and from the water rushing back and forth over it from gigantic tsunamis and their ricocheting— the result of the huge and sudden displacement of massive amount of water. The result of all these activities was huge land mass jotting out of the water and firmly and securely connected to the sea bed from where it came.

Huge amounts of water were trapped in various channels within the newly formed earth crust that was now projecting out of the water, further cooling the crust. And the rest of the water on the surface is pushed to one side as land developed out of the water and increased in size and altitude; thereby giving rise to the result that God commanded.

The water trapped inside the cooled earth's crust would later produce springs, streams and rivers that would continue to contour the surface of the land, to create top soil through erosions; to water the fields and support plants growth; and to provide fresh drinking water for all things living on the surface of the earth.

The same water that was trapped in channels within earth's crust was also used by God during the time of Noah to completely submerge and utterly annihilate everything on the surface of the earth; and separated land from land, giving rise to the continents and islands that exist on the earth day, and some which had since been reclaimed by the rising sea.

Here is what Apostle Peter said about God creating the earth with water:

"Dear friends, this is now my second letter to you. I have written both of them as reminders to stimulate you to wholesome thinking. ² I want you to recall the words spoken in the past by the holy prophets and the command given by our Lord and Savior through your apostles.

³ Above all, you must understand that in the last days scoffers will come, scoffing and following their own evil desires. ⁴ They will say, "Where is this 'coming' he promised? Ever since our ancestors died, everything goes on as it has since the beginning of creation." ⁵ But they deliberately forget that long ago by God's word the heavens came into being and the earth was formed out of water and by water. ⁶ By these waters also the world of that time was deluged and destroyed. ⁷ By the same word the present heavens and earth are reserved for fire, being kept for the day of judgment and destruction of the ungodly.

⁸ But do not forget this one thing, dear friends: With the Lord a day is like a thousand years, and a thousand years are like a day. ⁹ The Lord is not slow in keeping his promise, as some understand slowness. Instead he is patient with you, not wanting anyone to perish, but everyone to come to repentance.

¹⁰ But the day of the Lord will come like a thief. The heavens will disappear with a roar; the elements will be destroyed by fire, and the earth and everything done in it will be laid bare.

¹¹ Since everything will be destroyed in this way, what kind of people ought you to be? You ought to live holy and *godly lives * —

__godly lives__ ¹² __as you look forward to the day of God and speed its coming__. That day will bring about the destruction of the heavens by fire, and the elements will melt in the heat. ¹³ __But in keeping with his promise we are looking forward to a new heaven and a new earth, where righteousness dwells__.

¹⁴ So then, dear friends, since you are looking forward to this, make every effort to be found spotless, blameless and at peace with him. ¹⁵ __Bear in mind that our Lord's patience means salvation,__ just as our dear brother Paul also wrote you with the wisdom that God gave him. ¹⁶ He writes the same way in all his letters, speaking in them of these matters. His letters contain some things that are hard to understand, which ignorant and unstable people distort, as they do the other Scriptures, to their own destruction.

¹⁷ __Therefore, dear friends, since you have been forewarned, be on your guard so that you may not be carried away by the error of the lawless and fall from your secure position.__ ¹⁸ __But grow in the grace and knowledge of our Lord and Savior Jesus Christ. To him be glory both now and forever! Amen.__" (2 Peter 3:1-18).

So please be assured that the earth being formless, empty and dark were, rather, planned steps of the creation process that God carried out to accomplish His desired design. And this is exactly what God was talking about in the Book of Job when He rebuked Job about Job's misstatements. And in these passages in Job God provided great details He did not provide in Genesis:

ABOUT THE NEWLY FORMED EARTH BEING EMPTY:

The earth was empty at Genesis 1:2 because God was still forming the earth and He was going t. use violent, explosive and destructive forces in the steps to come to get to His intended end products—the earth and the universe.

The violent volcanic eruptions and the gigantic tsunamis that resulted and helped cooled the earth's crust that rose from the water in the volcanos, were both highly destructive events that the earth needed to be empty when the happened. And after these violent activities were taken care of, God finally populated the earth with life.

God created:

- Water and the earth *(Genesis 1:1-2)*—**matter**—Day 1
- light (and '**time**' began) *(Genesis 1:3-5)*—*Day 1*
- gases— through ionization from 'The Light' *(Genesis 1:3-5)*—Day 1
- **space** by stretching a void under water *(Genesis 1:6-8)*—Day 2
- the earth's crust (land) and the sea *(Genesis 1:9-10)*—Day 3
- and plant life *(Genesis1:11-13)* —Day 3
- the **universe**—in the Big Bang *(Genesis 1:14-19)*—Day 4
- aquatic life and the birds *(Genesis 1:20-23)*—Day 5
- land animals on land *(Genesis 1:24-25)*—Day 6 ;
- and finally He created man and woman *(Genesis 1:26-31)*—Day 6
- God Rested *(Genesis 2:2)*—Day 7

Ifeanyi Chukwujama

Chapter 7

Conclusion - God First Created the Earth, And then He Created the Universe!

So there you have it. The Trinity and all the heavenly hosts were around before the earth was created. God started created water and a 'blob' of earth and He completely submersed it under water. Then He commanded for lights and His Son Jesus Christ who had life and light in Him became the light, kicking off the dawn of time.

The Next day—Day 2— God called for space and stretched it out Himself. And He called it heaven.

And on Day 3, God commanded for land to appear and be separated from the water to create land and sea. Land developed and was separated from the sea. This was achieved again through His Son Jesus Christ.

On Day 4, God again commanded for lights in the firmament of heaven and what is today being talked about as the Big Band happened. The light—Jesus Christ—who appeared on Day 1, cataclysmically dispersed as balls of fire throughout the space that God 'stretched' out on Day 2. This completes the birth of the universe that was started by God on Day 2 when He created space to accommodate the dispersed energies of Day 4. The stars, the sun, the moon and all the other celestial bodies in space all came into existence on Day 4.

On Day 5 — the earth's sea were populated with living creatures. The living creatures of the sea were created with reproductive ability so they could replicate and expand in population. Birds emerged and took flight. The birds of the air were created with reproductive ability so they could replicate and expand in population. God blessed all of them to increase and multiply.

On Day 6 — the land was populated with living creatures of every kind—livestock, creatures that move along the ground, and wild animals.

And God created man in His own Image and gave man dominion over everything He had created on the earth: *"Then God said, "Let us make mankind in our image, in our likeness, so that they may rule over the fish in the sea and the birds in the sky, over the livestock and all the wild animals, and over all the creatures that move along the ground."*

[27] So God created mankind in his own image,
in the image of God he created them;
male and female he created them.

[28] God blessed them and said to them, "Be fruitful and increase in number; fill the earth and subdue it. Rule over the fish in the sea and the birds in the sky and over every living creature that moves on the ground."

[29] Then God said, "I give you every seed-bearing plant on the face of the whole earth and every tree that has fruit with seed in it. They will be yours for food. [30] And to all the beasts of the earth and all the birds in the sky and all the creatures that move along the ground—everything that has the breath of life in it—I give every green plant for food." And it was so." (Genesis 1:27-30).

On Day 7 — God rested. *"Thus the heavens and the earth were completed in all their vast array. [2] By the seventh day God had finished the work he had been doing; so on*

142

the seventh day he rested from all his work. [3] Then God blessed the seventh day and made it holy, because on it he rested from all the work of creating that he had done." *(Genesis 2:1-3).*

Below is an internet excerpt about Stephen Hawking's book. Whether a lie is dutifully reported word for word or is sensationalized by media, especially when the media is doing what it does best—selling stories—it does not change the nature of the lie. A lie is a lie and an affront to God and the good people of the world.

Anyone who says that God should not be mentioned in the discussion of creation is deluded. It is like saying that a man is a man without his head. Well if you remove the head, the man is no more—end of story. It is the same way with creation. No discussion of the creation of the universe has any truth in it if God is removed from it. It then becomes a figure of the imagination of whoever pieced together the story. And such is the case with Stephen Hawking.

We do not have the power and the authority to decide in what we want to involve God and in what we can keep Him out. God is intimate in our lives because He occupies every cell in each and every one of us and intrinsically controls all our thoughts and actions. God is always relevant in everything we do and talk about in our lives and He commands that we treat Him as such or face consequences. The Bible says: *"In all thy ways acknowledge him, and he shall direct thy paths."* *(Proverbs 3:6).*

"Hear, ye that are far off, what I have done; and, ye that are near, acknowledge my might." *(Isaiah 33:13).*

"Whosoever denieth the Son, the same hath not the Father: he that acknowledgeth the Son hath the Father also." *(1 John 2:23).*

"You live in the midst of deception; in their deceit they refuse to acknowledge me," declares the Lord." (Jeremiah 9:6).

"Pour out your wrath on the nations that do not acknowledge you, on the peoples who do not call on your name. For they have devoured Jacob; they have devoured him completely and destroyed his homeland." (Jeremiah 10:25).

"It is written: "'As surely as I live,' says the Lord, 'every knee will bow before me; every tongue will acknowledge God."" (Romans 14:11).

So, I hope that someone would be kind and pass this book to Stephen Hawking and his colleagues who continue to discuss matters they have no real knowledge about; but continue to sell their speculations as the truth, to the point of insulting the living God who single-handedly made the universe and the earth and everything in them. Here is the write up about hawking's book:

The Grand Design by Stephen Hawking and Leonard Mlodinow

Hawking and Mlodinow's new theory is about life, the universe and everything – except God

For those who have spent the last couple of weeks on a caving holiday or who have been on a visit to the glaciers of Svalbard, the news that <u>Stephen Hawking</u> *has published a new book – his first in a decade – may come as a surprise. For the rest of humanity, however, the information will by now seem as stale as a day-old pizza. Certainly, the blizzard of front-page stories that has greeted publication of the first extracts from The Grand Design has been extraordinary and, over the past two weeks, has given the scientist the kind of coverage that modern authors would sell their souls for (though for Tony Blair, this may be too late).*

"Hawking: God did not create universe", the Times announced on its front page, a splash story that was followed up for several days with as much furious religious reaction that the paper's writers could muster. Other media outlets followed suit – "Bang goes God, says Hawking", the Star announced – while rabbis, archbishops and religious historians filled letters pages and comment slots with waves of apoplectic outrage.

It has been a dispiriting experience. Setting religion against science, as the media has quite deliberately done in this case, achieves little for our attempts to understand the complexities of modern cosmology, the specific aim of Hawking and Mlodinow's book. Worse, the furore suggests that at the beginning of the 21st century, in our apparently rational, secular society, the declaration by a leading scientist that God was not involved in the universe's creation is deemed to be newsworthy and deserving of front-page headlines in national newspapers.

Nothing could be further from the truth, of course. Like most other physicists, Hawking has never expressed a need for God in his equations and has only made previous mentions to tease his readers. Fortunately, most of them have had the wit to appreciate this point. In fact, there is hardly a mention of a deity in The Grand Design. In the opening pages, there are a few mentions of clerical attempts in the middle ages to make philosophical sense of the heavens and that is about it – until we reach the last chapter.

"Spontaneous creation is the reason there is something rather than nothing, why the universe exists, why we exist," Hawking and Mlodinow announce at this point. "It is not necessary to invoke God to light the blue touch paper and set the universe going."

And that is just about it. The rest of the book is an attempt to account for the strange nature of reality as revealed by astronomers and physicists; to reconcile the apparent absurdities of quantum mechanics with the mind-stretching features of special and general relativity; and to explain why the forces of nature are apparently fine-tuned to allow the evolution of complex creatures such as ourselves. As Hawking and Mlodinow note, only the tiniest altering of the constants that control nuclear synthesis in stars would produce a universe with no carbon and no oxygen and therefore no humans.

"Our universe and its laws appear to have a design that both is tailor-made to support us and, if we are to exist, leaves little room for alternation," they state. "That is not easily explained, and raises the natural question of why it is that way." The answer, the authors say, lies with M-theory. (The M apparently stands for "master, miracle, or mystery". The authors are unsure which.) The vital point is that M-theory allows for the existence of 11 dimensions of spacetime that contains not just vibrating strings of matter but also "point particles, two-dimensional membranes, three-dimensional blobs and other objects that are more difficult to picture." Simple, really.

Crucially the laws of M-theory allow for an unimaginably large number of different universes. Thus we exist because the laws of our particular universe just happen to be tuned to the exact parameters that permit the existence of hydrogen, oxygen, carbon and other key atoms and which also generate laws that allow these entities to interact in ways that build up complex chemical combinations. Other universes are not so lucky.

M-theory is the unified theory of physics that Einstein was hoping to find, state the authors, and if it is confirmed by observation, it will be the successful conclusion to a search that was begun by the ancient Greeks when they started to puzzle about the nature of reality. "We will have found the grand design," Hawking and Mlodinow conclude.

It is all entertaining stuff, skilfully assembled and described in a fairly droll manner. The wave-particle duality of particles is described as being as foreign as drinking a chunk of sandstone, for example. The book is also commendably brief and by and large illuminating about the complexities of modern cosmology.

So read it to understand the universe. But if it is God you are after, my advice is to steer clear.

Here is a word for the world's community of science and astronomy: God is never angry at any man or woman for pursuing knowledge and for working hard trying to improve their lives or those of others. God actually blesses those who do these.

My revelation has uncovered more facts which God recorded on the first page of the Bible for those of us interested in pursuing true science. Science is not something that man concocted. Science is an approach to knowledge and was put together by God Himself; used by God Himself in designing and building the grandest project any being would undertake under the sun; and handed down to mankind to help us build our world and lives.

Science is good because God designed it and makes it available to the world. God used science to put together everything we see today, including us. God led us to science otherwise we would not have been able to acquire it. He wanted us to use it to progress our lives on earth—not to use it to increase our errors and get us lost in them.

Incorrect assumptions and extrapolations only lead to incorrect and even dangerous results and consequences which bring humanity closer and closer to its ultimate demise. God talks about the passing away of the current world and the current universe, not because

God lacks the power and good will to continue them; but because God already knew that man could not maintain straight ways but will always be chasing after vanity.

It may not be our generation if we become wise and obey God. But it will be a generation of humanity period. And that generation would get here and it will utterly hate God, confront God and resist God. And the end will come. But we can help delay the inevitable and give our children a better chance to survive and prosper God's way.

We do not understand how intimately and rigidly God controls everything in our lives, big or small. Nothing we do affects God in any way or form. But everything we do affects our fellow human being who God put in the world with us. God does not fight anyone, rather He allows anybody who chooses to remain out of line to suffer in the confusion of his own mind.

Any obedience on our part is hope for the next generation and possibly generations after them. We can let revival break out in this generation just like it did at Nineveh in the time of Jonah and God withdrew His wrath which would have overrun the people within forty days. The whole city was saved for another 150 years until another generation who did not know God brought back the wickedness of their fathers and were utterly destroyed. We have the power and it is very simple. Obey God and live!

Now let us all go back to work because we have much science to do. But let us do it with faith in God; love and respect for Jesus Christ and humanity; and purpose and compassion for mankind. And God will reward us abundantly as He promised.

When I first got the revelation from God, I was not sure why it was given to me and what I had to do with it. Then, I remembered Apostle Peter and the Gentile centurion: At first, Peter was unsure as to why he was summoned. But once he got to Cornelius, he realized what he was sent there to do. And just like Peter, I realized that the revelation I was given was to help reconcile science to God. Therefore, let us all work together to make this a reality so we can please God and activate His immeasurable power in our lives.

Ifeanyi Chukwujama

Chapter 8

Warning to the World

[36] "The king will do as he pleases. He will exalt and magnify himself above every god and will say unheard-of things against the God of gods. He will be successful until the time of wrath is completed, for what has been determined must take place. [37] He will show no regard for the gods of his ancestors or for the one desired by women, nor will he regard any god, but will exalt himself above them all. [38] Instead of them, he will honor a god of fortresses; a god unknown to his ancestors he will honor with gold and silver, with precious stones and costly gifts. [39] He will attack the mightiest fortresses with the help of a foreign god and will greatly honor those who acknowledge him. He will make them rulers over many people and will distribute the land at a price.

[40] "At the time of the end the king of the South will engage him in battle, and the king of the North will storm out against him with chariots and cavalry and a great fleet of ships. He will invade many countries and sweep through them like a flood. [41] He will also invade the Beautiful Land. Many countries will fall, but Edom, Moab and the leaders of Ammon will be delivered from his hand. [42] He will extend his power over many countries; Egypt will not escape. [43] He will gain control of the treasures of gold and silver and all the riches of Egypt, with the Libyans and Cushites in submission. [44] But reports from the east and the north will alarm him, and he will set out in a great rage to destroy and annihilate many. [45] He will pitch his royal tents between the seas at the beautiful holy mountain. Yet he will come to his end, and no one will help him.

In the Book of Isaiah God assured us:

"Remember this, keep it in mind,
take it to heart, you rebels.
⁹ Remember the former things, those of long ago;
I am God, and there is no other;
I am God, and there is none like me.
¹⁰ I make known the end from the beginning,
from ancient times, what is still to come.
I say, 'My purpose will stand,
and I will do all that I please.'
¹¹ From the east I summon a bird of prey;
from a far-off land, a man to fulfill my purpose.
What I have said, that I will bring about;
what I have planned, that I will do." (Isaiah 46:8-11).

"Now then, listen, you lover of pleasure,
lounging in your security
and saying to yourself,
'I am, and there is none besides me.
I will never be a widow
or suffer the loss of children.'
⁹ Both of these will overtake you
in a moment, on a single day:
loss of children and widowhood.
They will come upon you in full measure,
in spite of your many sorceries
and all your potent spells.
¹⁰ You have trusted in your wickedness
and have said, 'No one sees me.'
Your wisdom and knowledge mislead you
when you say to yourself,
'I am, and there is none besides me.'
¹¹ Disaster will come upon you,
and you will not know how to conjure it away.
A calamity will fall upon you
that you cannot ward off with a ransom;
a catastrophe you cannot foresee
will suddenly come upon you.

¹² "Keep on, then, with your magic spells
and with your many sorceries,

*which you have labored at since childhood.
Perhaps you will succeed,
    perhaps you will cause terror.
¹³ All the counsel you have received has only worn you
out!
    Let your astrologers come forward,
those stargazers who make predictions month by month,
    let them save you from what is coming upon you.
¹⁴ Surely they are like stubble;
    the fire will burn them up.
They cannot even save themselves
    from the power of the flame.
These are not coals for warmth;
    this is not a fire to sit by.
¹⁵ That is all they are to you—
    these you have dealt with
    and labored with since childhood.
All of them go on in their error;
    there is not one that can save you." (Isaiah 47:8-15).*

And nothing has changed since God gave mankind
the assurance. It still stands and will stand until God
accomplishes His purpose.

*"Make every effort to live in peace with everyone and to
be holy; without holiness no one will see the Lord. ¹⁵ See
to it that no one falls short of the grace of God and that no
bitter root grows up to cause trouble and defile many.
¹⁶ See that no one is sexually immoral, or is godless like
Esau, who for a single meal sold his inheritance rights as
the oldest son. ¹⁷ Afterward, as you know, when he
wanted to inherit this blessing, he was rejected. Even
though he sought the blessing with tears, he could not
change what he had done.*

The Mountain of Fear and the Mountain of Joy

*¹⁸ You have not come to a mountain that can be touched
and that is burning with fire; to darkness, gloom and
storm; ¹⁹ to a trumpet blast or to such a voice speaking*

153

words that those who heard it begged that no further word be spoken to them, ²⁰ because they could not bear what was commanded: "If even an animal touches the mountain, it must be stoned to death." ²¹ The sight was so terrifying that Moses said, "I am trembling with fear."

^{*22*} *But you have come to Mount Zion, to the city of the living God, the heavenly Jerusalem. You have come to thousands upon thousands of angels in joyful assembly, ²³ to the church of the firstborn, whose names are written in heaven. You have come to God, the Judge of all, to the spirits of the righteous made perfect, ²⁴ to Jesus the mediator of a new covenant, and to the sprinkled blood that speaks a better word than the blood of Abel.*

^{*25*} *See to it that you do not refuse him who speaks. If they did not escape when they refused him who warned them on earth, how much less will we, if we turn away from him who warns us from heaven? ²⁶ At that time his voice shook the earth, but now he has promised, "Once more I will shake not only the earth but also the heavens." ²⁷ The words "once more" indicate the removing of what can be shaken—that is, created things—so that what cannot be shaken may remain.*

^{*28*} *Therefore, since we are receiving a kingdom that cannot be shaken, let us be thankful, and so worship God acceptably with reverence and awe, ²⁹ for our "God is a consuming fire."* (Hebrews 12:14-29).

Nothing the world does today is a surprise to God. He knew all of it would come and the timing of them all was clear to His also. He knows the people He created and who is going to do what and He is keeping count. But like the Bible says God's patience means grace to mankind. We should all repent from our wrongdoings and seek God's face while it can be found.

I am inviting scientists and astronomers everywhere to go back to the foundation—the Bible, and piece things together from there. And finally the world would learn the truth and true purpose of our existence. It is not God's wish that humanity perishes. It is God's desire that all be save, and that is why He allows the world a long time to get it right. Let's all seek the truth and come to God. The whole truth is contained in the Bible waiting for us to discover it and praise God for His love and His wisdom!

It is **Matter**, then **time**, then **space**, then **universe**; and that is the truth about creation *(Genesis 1:1-19)!* Let us admit the truth of God and He will illuminate our hearts and lead us into more truths. The Big Bang did not create the earth, time or space *(Genesis 1:2-8)*. The Big bang created the universe to support the earth and showcase God's power for all humanity to see *(Genesis 1:14-19)*.

And plant life was already on the earth before the Big Bang took place. The earth and everything in it were protected by the Spirit of God from being destroyed in the Big Bang. That is part of the 'signs' mankind is supposed to see when it gazed into the shy.

If we discount the power of the Spirit of God, then we would never understand the force that holds everything down to the surface of the earth, and works in the same way on all the celestial bodies. We termed it gravity and have figured out a value for it but it is more than that. It is a living force that is actively applied by the Spirit of God. It is the same force that keeps things in orbit in space.

But we would never understand what is if we continue to discount God in science. For the glue to holds everything together on the earth and in the universe is unquestionable the Spirit of God which was infused into every atom of everything on the earth and in the universe *(Ephesians 4:4-10)*.

God is alive and as powerful as ever, and still at work. He had never ceased to operate from the time He created everything. See this passage from John: ***"In his defense Jesus said to them, 'My Father is always at his work to this very day, and I too am working.'"*** *(John 5:17)*. And He is not temperamental and as such would not act sooner than He swore to Himself because of human madness. His word will stand for ever.

While this new revelation will lead to rearranging our thoughts, and scrapping the Theory of Evolution and all the other discrepant theories and assumptions; it would help us line up a great majority of the scientific facts we conclusively know. It would invariably lead to a flood of new authentic discoveries.

If we remain on our current path of endless conjectures and science fictions, human civilization will meet its end earlier than God originally intended; because we will be robbing most of mankind of its faith in the only God of the universe. Science is vital in our lives, but science without the truth becomes science fiction and if not designated as such could lead to the eternal destruction of many souls.

God's way is not only the right way; God way is <u>the only way</u>: ***"For in him we live and move and have our being."*** *(Acts 17:28)*. Obey God and live!

INTERNET EXCERPTS:

1. <u>Christ says to be ready for His second coming:</u> *(Luke 17:1-37)*

   (http://www.biblegateway.com/passage/?search=Luke+17 &version=NIV)

   "Jesus said to his disciples: **"Things that cause people to stumble are bound to come, but woe to anyone through whom they come.** *² It would be better for them to be thrown into the sea with a millstone tied around their neck than to cause one of these little ones to stumble." (Luke 17:31-2)*

   ³ **"So watch yourselves. If your brother or sister sins against you, rebuke them; and if they repent, forgive them.** *⁴ Even if they sin against you seven times in a day and seven times come back to you saying 'I repent,' you must forgive them." (Luke 17:3-4)*

   ⁵" The apostles said to the Lord, "Increase our faith!" (Luke 17:5)

   ⁶ "He replied, "If you have faith as small as a mustard seed, you can say to this mulberry tree, 'Be uprooted and planted in the sea,' and it will obey you." (Luke 17:6)

   ⁷ "Suppose one of you has a servant plowing or looking after the sheep. Will he say to the servant when he comes in from the field, 'Come along now and sit down to eat'? ⁸ Won't he rather say, 'Prepare my supper, get yourself ready and wait on me while I eat and drink; after that you may eat and drink'? ⁹ Will he thank the servant because he did what he was told to do? ¹⁰ So you also, when you have done everything you were told to do, should say, 'We

are unworthy servants; we have only done our duty.'"
(Luke 17:7-10)

Jesus Heals Ten Men With Leprosy

[11] *"Now on his way to Jerusalem, Jesus traveled along the border between Samaria and Galilee.* [12] *As he was going into a village, ten men who had leprosy[b] met him. They stood at a distance* [13] *and called out in a loud voice, 'Jesus, Master, have pity on us!'"* *(Luke 17:11-13)*

[14] *"When he saw them, he said, "Go, show yourselves to the priests." And as they went, they were cleansed".* *(Luke 17:14)*

[15] *"One of them, when he saw he was healed, came back, praising God in a loud voice.* [16] *He threw himself at Jesus' feet and thanked him—and he was a Samaritan."* *(Luke 17:15-16)*

[17] *"Jesus asked, "Were not all ten cleansed? Where are the other nine?* [18] *Has no one returned to give praise to God except this foreigner?"* [19] *Then he said to him, 'Rise and go; your faith has made you well.'"* *(Luke 17:17-19)*

The Coming of the Kingdom of God

[20] *Once, on being asked by the Pharisees when the kingdom of God would come, Jesus replied, "The coming of the kingdom of God is not something that can be observed,* [21] *nor will people say, 'Here it is,' or 'There it is,' because the kingdom of God is in your midst."* *(Luke 17:20-21)*

[22] *"Then he said to his disciples, "The time is coming when you will long to see one of the days of the Son of Man, but you will not see it.* [23] *People will tell you, 'There he is!' or 'Here he is!' Do not go running off after them.*

^{24} For the Son of Man in his day will be like the lightning, which flashes and lights up the sky from one end to the other. ^{25} But first he must suffer many things and be rejected by this generation." (Luke 17:22-25)

^{26} "Just as it was in the days of Noah, so also will it be in the days of the Son of Man. ^{27} People were eating, drinking, marrying and being given in marriage up to the day Noah entered the ark. Then the flood came and destroyed them all." (Luke 17:26-27)

^{28} "It was the same in the days of Lot. People were eating and drinking, buying and selling, planting and building. ^{29} But the day Lot left Sodom, fire and sulfur rained down from heaven and destroyed them all." (Luke 17:28-29)

^{30} "It will be just like this on the day the Son of Man is revealed. ^{31} On that day no one who is on the housetop, with possessions inside, should go down to get them. Likewise, no one in the field should go back for anything. **^{32} Remember Lot's wife!^{33} Whoever tries to keep their life will lose it, and whoever loses their life will preserve it.** *^{34} I tell you, on that night two people will be in one bed; one will be taken and the other left. ^{35} Two women will be grinding grain together; one will be taken and the other left." (Luke 17:30-36)*

^{37} "Where, Lord?" they asked.

He replied, **'Where there is a dead body, there the vultures will gather.'"** *(Luke 17:37)*

2. *The events of the Bible were well documented and* **heralded** *(Psalm 78:1-72) among many other passages in the Bible.*

(http://www.biblegateway.com/passage/?search=psalm+78&version=NIV)

A *maskil*[a] of Asaph.

[1] My people, hear my teaching;
    listen to the words of my mouth.
[2] I will open my mouth with a parable;
    I will utter hidden things, things from of old—
[3] things we have heard and known,
    things our ancestors have told us.
[4] We will not hide them from their descendants;
    we will tell the next generation
the praiseworthy deeds of the LORD,
    his power, and the wonders he has done.
[5] He decreed statutes for Jacob
    and established the law in Israel,
which he commanded our ancestors
    to teach their children,
[6] so the next generation would know them,
    even the children yet to be born,
    and they in turn would tell their children.
[7] Then they would put their trust in God
    and would not forget his deeds
    but would keep his commands.
[8] They would not be like their ancestors—
    a stubborn and rebellious generation,
whose hearts were not loyal to God,
    whose spirits were not faithful to him.

[9] The men of Ephraim, though armed with bows,
    turned back on the day of battle;
[10] they did not keep God's covenant
    and refused to live by his law.

¹¹ They forgot what he had done,
   the wonders he had shown them.
¹² He did miracles in the sight of their ancestors
   in the land of Egypt, in the region of Zoan.
¹³ He divided the sea and led them through;
   he made the water stand up like a wall.
¹⁴ He guided them with the cloud by day
   and with light from the fire all night.
¹⁵ He split the rocks in the wilderness
   and gave them water as abundant as the seas;
¹⁶ he brought streams out of a rocky crag
   and made water flow down like rivers.

¹⁷ But they continued to sin against him,
   rebelling in the wilderness against the Most High.
¹⁸ They willfully put God to the test
   by demanding the food they craved.
¹⁹ They spoke against God;
   they said, "Can God really
   spread a table in the wilderness?
²⁰ True, he struck the rock,
   and water gushed out,
   streams flowed abundantly,
but can he also give us bread?
   Can he supply meat for his people?"
²¹ When the LORD heard them, he was furious;
   his fire broke out against Jacob,
   and his wrath rose against Israel,
²² for they did not believe in God
   or trust in his deliverance.
²³ Yet he gave a command to the skies above
   and opened the doors of the heavens;
²⁴ he rained down manna for the people to eat,
   he gave them the grain of heaven.
²⁵ Human beings ate the bread of angels;
   he sent them all the food they could eat.
²⁶ He let loose the east wind from the heavens
   and by his power made the south wind blow.
²⁷ He rained meat down on them like dust,
   birds like sand on the seashore.
²⁸ He made them come down inside their camp,
   all around their tents.

²⁹ They ate till they were gorged—
   he had given them what they craved.
³⁰ But before they turned from what they craved,
   even while the food was still in their mouths,
³¹ God's anger rose against them;
   he put to death the sturdiest among them,
   cutting down the young men of Israel.

³² In spite of all this, they kept on sinning;
   in spite of his wonders, they did not believe.
³³ So he ended their days in futility
   and their years in terror.
³⁴ Whenever God slew them, they would seek him;
   they eagerly turned to him again.
³⁵ They remembered that God was their Rock,
   that God Most High was their Redeemer.
³⁶ But then they would flatter him with their mouths,
   lying to him with their tongues;
³⁷ their hearts were not loyal to him,
   they were not faithful to his covenant.
³⁸ Yet he was merciful;
   he forgave their iniquities
   and did not destroy them.
Time after time he restrained his anger
   and did not stir up his full wrath.
³⁹ He remembered that they were but flesh,
   a passing breeze that does not return.

⁴⁰ How often they rebelled against him in the wilderness
   and grieved him in the wasteland!
⁴¹ Again and again they put God to the test;
   they vexed the Holy One of Israel.
⁴² They did not remember his power—
   the day he redeemed them from the oppressor,
⁴³ the day he displayed his signs in Egypt,
   his wonders in the region of Zoan.
⁴⁴ He turned their river into blood;
   they could not drink from their streams.
⁴⁵ He sent swarms of flies that devoured them,
   and frogs that devastated them.
⁴⁶ He gave their crops to the grasshopper,
   their produce to the locust.

⁴⁷ He destroyed their vines with hail
  and their sycamore-figs with sleet.
⁴⁸ He gave over their cattle to the hail,
  their livestock to bolts of lightning.
⁴⁹ He unleashed against them his hot anger,
  his wrath, indignation and hostility—
  a band of destroying angels.
⁵⁰ He prepared a path for his anger;
  he did not spare them from death
  but gave them over to the plague.
⁵¹ He struck down all the firstborn of Egypt,
  the firstfruits of manhood in the tents of Ham.
⁵² But he brought his people out like a flock;
  he led them like sheep through the wilderness.
⁵³ He guided them safely, so they were unafraid;
  but the sea engulfed their enemies.
⁵⁴ And so he brought them to the border of his holy land,
  to the hill country his right hand had taken.
⁵⁵ He drove out nations before them
  and allotted their lands to them as an inheritance;
  he settled the tribes of Israel in their homes.

⁵⁶ But they put God to the test
  and rebelled against the Most High;
  they did not keep his statutes.
⁵⁷ Like their ancestors they were disloyal and faithless,
  as unreliable as a faulty bow.
⁵⁸ They angered him with their high places;
  they aroused his jealousy with their idols.
⁵⁹ When God heard them, he was furious;
  he rejected Israel completely.
⁶⁰ He abandoned the tabernacle of Shiloh,
  the tent he had set up among humans.
⁶¹ He sent the ark of his might into captivity,
  his splendor into the hands of the enemy.
⁶² He gave his people over to the sword;
  he was furious with his inheritance.
⁶³ Fire consumed their young men,
  and their young women had no wedding songs;
⁶⁴ their priests were put to the sword,
  and their widows could not weep.

[65] Then the Lord awoke as from sleep,
  as a warrior wakes from the stupor of wine.
[66] He beat back his enemies;
  he put them to everlasting shame.
[67] Then he rejected the tents of Joseph,
  he did not choose the tribe of Ephraim;
[68] but he chose the tribe of Judah,
  Mount Zion, which he loved.
[69] He built his sanctuary like the heights,
  like the earth that he established forever.
[70] He chose David his servant
  and took him from the sheep pens;
[71] from tending the sheep he brought him
  to be the shepherd of his people Jacob,
  of Israel his inheritance.
[72] And David shepherded them with integrity of heart;
  with skillful hands he led them.

3. *Ionosphere*

(From Encylopedia.com)

- *"Sun's ultraviolet, x-ray, and corpuscular radiation, and partially by cosmic rays, resulting in ions and free electrons. The ionization process depends on many factors such as the Sun's activity (e.g., sunspot cycles), time (e.g., seasonal or daily changes), or geographical location (different at polar regions, mid-latitudes or equatorial zones).*
- *The ionosphere can be further divided into sub-regions according to their free electron density profile that indicates the degree of ionization, and these sub-regions are called the D, E, and F layers. The D layer is located lowest among them, and it does not have an exact starting point. It absorbs high-frequency radio waves, and exists mainly during the day. It weakens, then gradually even disappears at night, allowing radio waves to penetrate into a higher level of the ionosphere, where these waves are reflected back to Earth, then bounce again back into the ionosphere. This explains why AM radio signals from distant stations can easily be picked up at night, even from hundreds of*

miles. Above the D layer, the E layer (or Kennelly-Heaviside layer) can be found, which historically was the first one that was discovered. After sunset, it usually starts to weaken and by night, it also disappears. The E layer absorbs x rays, and it has its peak at about 65 mi (105 km). The F layer (or Appleton layer) can be found above the E layer, above 93 mi (150 km), and it has the highest concentration of charged particles. Although its structure changes during the day, the F layer is a relatively constant layer, where extreme ultra-violet radiation is absorbed. It has two parts: the lower F1 layer, and the higher and more electron-dense F2 layer.

- *The free electrons in the ionosphere allow good propagation of electromagnetic waves, and excellent radio communication. The ionosphere is also the home for the aurora, a light display mostly in the night sky of the polar areas, caused by excited and light-emitting particles entering the upper atmosphere."*

ABOUT THE AUTHOR

It is by the power of God through faith in His Son Jesus Christ that this book was written. I have been on a spiritual journey for most of my adult life, trying to figure out who I am and why I am the way I am.

I have a Bachelor's Degree in Chemical Engineering worked in various engineering capacity in several pharmaceutical and bio-tech companies. But the love of God, the yawning for God's guidance, His direction and His protection in my life, and the pursuit of the truth of God; have dominated most of my existence. God was introduced into my life at a very early stage.

I was sickly as a baby that my parents were afraid they were going to lose me. Growing up I could never remember my father laying a finger on me throughout my life. So one day I asked him why? Not because I enjoyed being hit but because other grownups have hit me and kids all around me were treated the same way in admonition.

My father laughed so hard and after a while, he said told me that he once hit me, when I was a child, and I cried uncontrollably for a long time and had a seizure that they thought they were going to lose me. After, that he swore never to touch me again and he had not since. I say to myself: 'way to go—if you want nobody to bother you, get sick and scare them away'.

And after those early years of being sick all the time, I was in great health for as long as I can remember. I cannot remember ever being taken to the hospital because I was sick. Just occasional flu here and there! And I attribute the good health to the Lord who promises to keep us in good health and abundance if we would listen to Him and do as He commanded. I will be lying to myself and to my readers if I claim that I have always kept the commands of Jesus Christ.

Then again, it is not my ability to keep all of God's commands that is demanded of me—and of every person in the world. It is my desire and determination to keep the commands that endears me to God. God knows that on my own, I could do only so much, and so He demands that I surrender my life to Him so He could lead me in the ways I should go. And when I surrendered and made Jesus Christ everything I need in life, He has mercy on me and overlooks the errors I make every now and then. That is all God is asking for from any of us.

That is why the Bible says: ***"Now all has been heard; here is the conclusion of the matter: Fear God and keep his commandments, for <u>this is the duty of all mankind</u>." (Ecclesiastes 12:13).*** The only duty of man is to determine to obey God and keep His commandments. It is the determination to do what God commands that counts. In essence, God examines your intent your because your obedience starts with your intent, and carries through in your actions. So if your intent is good, your action is bound to be good; but if your intent is not firm and resolute, your action could be anything but the right thing.

When I started receiving revelations from God, I knew there was nothing else in the world that I needed more than working for God. The messages were coming to me rapidly and I was writing feverishly, going for stretches of time frequently without a break. The more I write, the more I receive and the more I want to continue to write. But nobody knows who I am and what I have to say so my books remain in obscurity. I kept saying to myself that it is God who gave me the messages and it is God who will ensure that the messages get out, so I kept waiting.

Then I asked God for music to help me spread the word and immediately He answered and I started writing songs and singing the messages in my songs, while at the same time writing more books. Then I received the revelations in this book. First I was shocked that they were revealed to me. Then I realized that together, they were a confirmation for all the messages in my previous books and the music.

In my excitement, I wrote this book in the shortest amount of time it had taken me to write the previous book which further strengthens my belief that when God gives, He pours it on, and I am forever thankful to Him for all His goodness to me. For the Bible reminds us that ***"the kingdom of God is not a matter of talk but of power."*** *(1 Corinthians 4:20).* To affirm that what you hear from the Bible is true, put it into practice and see if it does not lead to what the Bible promises it will lead to. God does not make empty promises. If you do as He says to do, He responds as He promises to respond, and in multiples. Resolve to serve God and experience His love and His goodness.

He made man, the heavens and the earth; and put his power on display throughout the universe. He is God and there is no other!

Other Titles from This Author:

- Who Is God!
- Christianity Is Not A Religion!
- The Singleness of God
- What Is Love?
- Overcoming Your Trials
- Live the Abundant Life
- Science, Evolution and God
- Reflections of Life
- Christ Is In Everyone!
- The Rapture, The Tribulations and the Church

www.ingramcontent.com/pod-product-compliance
Lightning Source LLC
Chambersburg PA
CBHW031533040426
42445CB00010B/518